FILMMAKERS SEF
edited by
ANTHONY SLIDE

Elisabeth Welch

Soft Lights and Sweet Music

Stephen Bourne

Filmmakers Series, No. 120

THE SCARECROW PRESS, INC.
Lanham, Maryland • Toronto • Oxford
2005

SCARECROW PRESS, INC.

Published in the United States of America
by Scarecrow Press, Inc.
A wholly owned subsidiary of
The Rowman & Littlefield Publishing Group, Inc.
4501 Forbes Boulevard, Suite 200, Lanham, Maryland 20706
www.scarecrowpress.com

PO Box 317
Oxford
OX2 9RU, UK

British Library Cataloguing in Publication Information Available

Library of Congress Cataloging-in-Publication Data

Bourne, Stephen.
  Elisabeth Welch : soft lights and sweet music / Stephen Bourne.
    p. cm. — (Filmmakers ; no. 120)
  Includes bibliographical references (p.   ), discography (p.   ), filmography (p.   ), and
index.
  ISBN 0-8108-5413-9 (pbk. : alk. paper)
  1. Welch, Elisabeth. 2. African American singers—Biography. 3. African American
actresses—Biography. I. Title. II. Series: Filmmakers series ; no. 120.
ML420.W36B68 2005
782.42164'092—dc22
                                                                2005000059

∞™ The paper used in this publication meets the minimum requirements of
American National Standard for Information Sciences—Permanence of Paper for
Printed Library Materials, ANSI/NISO Z39.48-1992.
Manufactured in the United States of America.

Contents

~

Foreword
Ned Sherrin

The Oldest hath borne most: we that are young
Shall never see so much or live so long.

I'm not sure that Lis would like to be remembered alongside King Lear, but for most of a hundred years she brought unique style, musicianship, crystal-clear diction, and sophistication to the art of popular song. In her hands it was high art.

She was born in 1904. Her father John, a chauffeur and gardener in New Jersey, was half Native American, half African American. Her mother was half Irish, half Scots. Hence her objection to Paul Robeson when they were filming *Song of Freedom*. He wanted her to make a stand for "your people." Lis said, "Paul, I can't make a stand for *all* of them!"

She complained to her mother that there was no Jewish blood in that rich cocktail. "Oh yes there is," said her mother. "You were very weak when you were born. The doctor blew air into your mouth to get you going, and he was Jewish!"

Her young life was spent on the west side of Manhattan, where the Lincoln Centre now stands. Her "loud alto" stood out in the Episcopalian church choir. At school she was in *H.M.S. Pinafore*. What did she play? Stupidly, I never asked. The year 1923 saw her on Broadway, in *Runnin' Wild*. She introduced the "Charleston," a dance that caught on, with a song she despised. Her Presbyterian father was shocked and disappeared from her young life. His last recorded words were, "Girlie's gone on the boards. She's lost!"

The rest of the decade is a kaleidoscope of Josephine Baker, Bojangles, New York, Paris, Moulin Rouge, Chez Florence, Le Boeuf sur le Toit, Bricktop, Mabel Mercer, Gertrude Stein, Cocteau, Picasso, Scott Fitzgerald. Then came her defining moment.

Irving Berlin heard her sing at the Royal Box cabaret. There was trouble with his friend Cole Porter's revue *The New Yorkers*. Kathryn Crawford, backed by The Three Girl Friends, was performing "Love for Sale," a song condemned as in "the worst possible taste." Miss Crawford, the Girl Friends, and a street sign reading "Madison Avenue" were removed, and the location was changed to Harlem and the Cotton Club. On Berlin's recommendation Lis triumphed as the first solo singer of that classic song.

After 156 performances she headed back to Paris. Porter was cooking up *Nymph Errant* for C. B. Cochran. He wrote "Solomon" for her. At last, she came to London. Before *Nymph Errant* Cochran allowed her to introduce "Stormy Weather" in a revue, *Dark Doings*, at the Leicester Square Theatre. She stopped the show with "Solomon" at the Adelphi. According to the leading critic James Agate, in a review she loved to quote, it was "a hot ditty, bawled by a *Negresse Soi-dissant*."

She went to work with Ivor Novello in *Glamorous Night* and *Arc de Triomphe*, introducing his "Far Away in Shanty Town" and "Dark Music."

She had impeccable taste in picking out a song. On a raid for new material in New York she discovered "As Time Goes By," about to be forgotten in a revue, *Everyone's Welcome*—to which, sadly, nobody came. She kept it alive for ten years until *Casablanca* picked it up.

She headlined at the London Palladium and on the Moss Empire's circuit billed as "Syncopating Songstress," "Sepia Songstress," and, for a time, "Mistress of Song." While appearing in a Birmingham theatre she overheard a girl in a queue say to her companion, "Mistress of Song. I told you she was kept by a Chinaman."

During the war she chose to stay in Britain, starring at the Palladium with Tommy Trinder and touring the troops in the Mediterranean and North Africa with John Gielgud, Edith Evans, Beatrice Lillie, and Jeanne de Casalis. Gielgud recorded, "You could hear a pin-drop when she was singing. When she stopped all hell broke loose."

After the war she continued to pick songs wisely, introducing Edith Piaf's "La Vie en Rose" in one of the three Laurier Lister revues in which she starred.

She forged new friendships with Millicent Martin in Peter Greenwell's *The Crooked Mile* and with Cleo Laine in *Cindy-Ella*. Cleo stayed with her in Capener's Close and sat up all hours hearing her lines.

It was always hard getting words into that old head, but once a song was there it stuck, and when it came out it was perfectly phrased. Lying back on her bed at Denville Hall in her late nineties she ran through verse and chorus, a cappella, of "Why Was I Born," "What Is This Thing Called Love?" and Novello's "Far Away in Shanty Town," without missing a syllable.

We worked together off and on from the late 1950s. Her approach to "Love for Sale" changed. "I used to sing it as a tart. Now I'll do it as a Madame advertising young love for sale."

I arranged a last-minute audition for her for Bob Fosse. The role was the Queen Mother in *Pippin*—her first audition in fifty years. Fosse was gracious. "What will you sing, Miss Welch?" "A little song Cole Porter wrote for me." She got the part.

There were two hip operations and then the wonderful renaissance of the 1980s—Derek Jarman's *The Tempest*, David Kernan's *Kern Goes to Hollywood* (she was mugged during the run but insisted on playing at the Donmar Theatre the next night), Bobby Short's *Black Broadway*, and finally with her one-woman show, a prophet in her own country.

In the *New York Times* Frank Rich claimed her as a national treasure. "The government should take steps to prevent her from leaving the country." She made her first visits to Los Angeles and Australia. She sang to four and a half thousand people in Russia.

At home she was tireless in performing in charity concerts for AIDS victims. The apotheosis was a programme honouring her at the Lyric in 1992.

Finally Kenneth Partridge, aided and abetted by Moyra Fraser and Wendy Toye, kidnapped her and spirited her away on a visit to Denville Hall. After a look around, on the way home they asked, "When would you like to move in, Lis?" "Tomorrow!"

Only then was the long-kept secret of her age resolved. Kenneth said to her brother, John, "We had to move her. Let's face it, she's well over 80." "80!" said brother John, "Girlie is 93."

At Denville Hall she was loved and cherished. Her habits had always been nocturnal. One night she went wandering in her bright red dressing gown. She landed in the wrong bedroom. As she climbed into the wrong bed the regular inhabitant of the room thought Father Christmas had arrived. When she found out who it was she phoned her daughter and said, "Guess who's in my bed?" By that time Lis was fast asleep.

Everyone who knew Lis has their memories of her—that great, glamorous, earthy, lovely, cussed, cantankerous, opinionated, beguiling, demanding, easy, night-owl, gourmet, fine-wine-appreciating, wonderful woman. The talented, tasteful, musicianly interpreter of only the best in popular song.

She liked to close rehearsals, conversations, even arguments with a simple "Amen."

So, "Amen, Lis."

Producer and broadcaster Ned Sherrin worked with Elisabeth many times from the late 1950s. Their collaborations included stage (Cindy-Ella, 1962), film (Girl Stroke Boy, 1971), and many television programmes, such as Take a Sapphire *(1966),* The Long Cocktail Party *(1966),* Cindy-Ella *(1966),* Song by Song by Cole Porter *(1980) and Ned's* This Is Your Life *(1995). In 1992 Ned hosted* A Time to Start Living, *an all-star tribute to Elisabeth at the Lyric Theatre.*

~

Acknowledgments

I would like to thank the following for their help and friendship: Iain Cameron Williams (author of *Underneath a Harlem Moon: The Harlem to Paris Years of Adelaide Hall*), Bill Egan (author of *Florence Mills: Harlem Jazz Queen*), Alexander Gleason (for his help with identifying the songs Elisabeth performed in her films), Derek Granger, Bryan Hammond (for his help with identifying Elisabeth's concert appearances and for sharing his memories of Elisabeth), Derek Hunt (for *Salute to Malta*), Delilah Jackson, Richard Mangan (Mander and Mitchenson Theatre Collection), Patrick Newley, Graham Nightingale, Richard Norman, Hugh Palmer (for his help with the Discography), Kenneth Partridge, Ken Sephton, Jim Simpson, Ned Sherrin, Anthony Slide, Aaron Smith, and Robert Taylor.

Thanks to the staff of Denville Hall for keeping Elisabeth safe and happy; to Elisabeth's friend Michael Alexander; to the Theatre Museum (London); to the British Film Institute (London); and to BBC Written Archives (Caversham).

Thanks to Stephen Sondheim for granting permission to quote his 1986 telegram; to the trustees of the Sir John Gielgud Charitable Trust for permission to include Sir John Gielgud's correspondence; and to Karl Magee, project archivist for the Lindsay Anderson Collection at the University of Sterling, for permission to include Lindsay Anderson's 1987 letter.

With the exception of Robert Taylor's 1996 photograph of Elisabeth and George Melly (thank you, Robert!), all the photographs in this book come from Elisabeth's private collection, now in the possession of the author.

Though every care has been taken, if, through inadvertence or failure to trace the present owners we have included any copyright material without acknowledgement or permission, we offer our apologies to all concerned.

This book is dedicated to the memory of my friend and "soul-mate" Sonia Pascal (1959–2004), who in 1982 made it possible for me to have my first article published. Without Sonia's interest in my work, and her encouragement, I would not have found the confidence to pursue a career as a writer and researcher.

~

Introduction

For six decades Elisabeth Welch was one of the most popular singers working in Britain and a permanent fixture on London's West End musical stage, from Cole Porter's *Nymph Errant* in 1933 to the all-star tribute concert *A Time to Start Living* in 1992. The star of the former was the legendary Gertrude Lawrence. The latter, a World AIDS Day Gala, featured the cream of British show business. Cleo Laine, Sally Ann Howes, Petula Clark, David Kernan, Elaine Delmar, Liz Robertson, Julia McKenzie, Millicent Martin, and the host, Ned Sherrin, were among those who paid tribute to Elisabeth, and they joined the audience to give her an unprecedented (as far as anyone there could remember) five standing ovations.

Elisabeth regarded herself as American by birth but English in thought and interest. London was her home for seventy years. She thus stood apart from other African American women entertainers of her generation, including the extrovert Josephine Baker and the dynamic, outspoken Lena Horne. However, when a curious journalist enquired about the singing technique she had sustained for over eighty years, her simple, direct reply was, "I have no technique. No art, no training. Nothing! Just myself. I describe myself as a singer of popular songs."

Born in New York of mixed parentage, Elisabeth was a trailblazer for black women in Britain in the 1930s and 1940s. At that time, Elisabeth was the most famous black woman in Britain and a sophisticated, stylish interpreter of popular songs. The British public was drawn to her beauty and elegance, her soft, lovely voice, and her perfect diction. In the 1930s the Jamaican-born

Pauline Henriques joined a drama course at the London Academy of Music and Dramatic Art. She recalled:

> I just adored Elisabeth Welch. I thought she was the most wonderful black person ever. She had grace and beauty, and a tremendous range in her singing voice. She could also act. So, of course, I modelled myself on her and dreamed that, maybe, one day I could be her understudy, but that dream was never realised. I understudied other people, including Georgia Burke in the London production of *Anna Lucasta* in 1947, but I never got to understudy Elisabeth Welch.

I first heard about Elisabeth from my mother. I couldn't have been more than seven or eight years old. It was sometime in the mid-1960s, and she was singing on the radio. My mother said, "That's Elisabeth Welch," and explained, "She's a famous singer. Before the war Aunt Esther made dresses for her. Now and again, when I was little, she took me to her house to deliver the dresses."

Aunt Esther, a black Londoner born just before the First World War, worked as a seamstress for sixty years, from the age of fourteen until she retired at the age of seventy-four. In 1935 she went to work for Miss Mary Taylor in Markham Square, off King's Road in Chelsea. She said, "That was a nice job, and Miss Taylor was very good to me. She lived upstairs with her boyfriend. He was an artist. I worked in the basement. It was mostly handwork, and I used all kinds of fabrics. I didn't use a sewing machine very much."

While Cole Porter and Ivor Novello wrote songs for Elisabeth, Aunt Esther made her dresses and delivered them, in person, to her home, a flat in Cottage Walk, off Sloane Street. Though both of them were Londoners, the worlds the two women inhabited couldn't have been farther apart. Unlike many of her black contemporaries, including my aunt, Elisabeth was largely protected from racism in the world of musical theatre.

Aunt Esther lived in a tight-knit, working-class community in Fulham, sharing a room with my great-grandmother in cramped conditions in a house without electricity, and with a lavatory in the back yard. Elisabeth's mews flat in an exclusive part of London included art deco furniture, a baby grand piano that held a delightful "Abdullah" doll given to her by Gertrude Lawrence when they opened together in *Nymph Errant*, and a bust of Elisabeth's friend Noël Coward by the artist and stage designer Gladys Calthrop.

Aunt Esther adored her: "She was elegant and a very classy lady. She appeared in shows in the West End and made films with Paul Robeson. I often listened to her singing on the wireless [radio]. Now and again Miss Taylor said, 'Go on, Esther, take this dress to her house for me.' Sometimes I took little Kathy [the author's mother] for company. So I met Elisabeth Welch. She was a lovely person and always treated me with kindness."

During the Second World War, the British government introduced conscription for single women, and Aunt Esther, who was unmarried, was informed she would have to leave Miss Taylor and undertake war work. At first she was employed at Brompton Hospital as a cleaner and fire watcher during air raids, but she later returned to being a seamstress in the hospital's linen room. Though she never saw Elisabeth Welch again, Aunt Esther was proud of her association with the famous singer and followed her career with interest. My aunt passed away on July 17, 1994, aged eighty-one.

On May 28, 1982, I met Elisabeth for the first time. The occasion was the closing night of her triumphant series of one-woman shows at the Riverside Studios in Hammersmith. I attended the concert, which, as promised in the programme, included songs by some of the great composers and lyricists of the twentieth century: Hoagy Carmichael, George Gershwin, Richard Rodgers and Lorenz Hart, Cole Porter and Ivor Novello. Each song was greeted by a rousing ovation from the audience. Elisabeth was on top form, and I was thrilled to be there.

After the concert I visited her crowded dressing-room. Feeling shy, I stood in a corner. One by one excited friends and fans greeted Elisabeth and expressed their joy at seeing her in performance and in person. In her diary entry for that evening she listed some of the famous names who had been in attendance: the lyricist Alan Jay Lerner (of My Fair Lady and Camelot fame); Anton Dolin, the dancer and former member of Diaghilev's Russian Ballet; the legendary actress and singer Evelyn "Boo" Laye, who had attended the opening night of Elisabeth's first West End success Nymph Errant in 1933; and the architect Sir Hugh Casson, then president of the Royal Academy. At that time I didn't know who they were. The only person I recognised was the openly gay artist and filmmaker Derek Jarman, who in 1979 had directed Elisabeth in an unusual screen version of William Shakespeare's The Tempest, in which she sang "Stormy Weather." He introduced her to an "artistic" looking young lad whom he described as "her latest fan."

One by one her friends and fans left. Finally Miss Welch spotted me, a young man hovering in the corner, too shy to approach her. Sensing my awkwardness, she called me to her. I introduced myself and handed her a letter. She took my hand, and I immediately felt at ease. "Cold hand, warm heart," she said, "I bet you're a Scorpio!" She was right. Some months later she responded to my letter and invited me to her home.

In 1959 Elisabeth had moved from Cottage Walk to nearby Capener's Close, off Kinnerton Street, in Knightsbridge. I discovered that her Kinnerton Street neighbours included, at one time or another, Lord Louis Mountbatten, opera singer Leontyne Price, actress Hermione Gingold, and film director Brian Desmond Hurst. On October 19, 1982, I found myself in her beautiful home, and, as I entered, what impressed me was that Elisabeth had kept most of the furnishings and elegance of the 1930s. After welcoming me, Elisabeth led me into her drawing-room, painted a dusky pink, and excused herself. While she disappeared into her kitchen, I made myself comfortable on her large sofa and admired a framed 1935 portrait of Elisabeth by Gerald Brockhurst. I then gazed in wonder at her baby grand piano (I had never seen one before), which had a large coffee-table book about Cole Porter resting on the top. I was also very impressed with Gladys Calthrop's bust of Noël Coward. By the side of the sofa was a large pile of music sheets. Elisabeth returned with a small tray of tea, biscuits, and cakes. "Help yourself," she said, and then we spent about an hour chatting about her career and some of the famous people she had encountered. I also enquired about the impressive portrait on the wall. "I was appearing in Ivor Novello's *Glamorous Night*," she explained. "Gerald Brockhurst saw me as the stowaway, and he said 'I want that look.'"

Elisabeth was full of joy and happiness and possessed a loud, impressive laugh. I warmed to her, and her laugh, immediately. She told me she loved to be with people who had a sense of humour; she was fun to be with and interesting to talk to. I felt that she wanted to be liked for herself, not for her public persona. I realised that Elisabeth responded well to people who were honest, straightforward, and just being themselves. I believe she found it difficult to relate to people who were "star struck" and in awe of her. It made her feel uncomfortable. I also discovered that Elisabeth was more interested in the person she was talking to than in talking about herself. So I gradually found myself talking about my work, family, and interests—and this is what made Elisabeth so special. She may have rubbed shoulders with the likes of Cole Porter, Charles B. Cochran, Noël Coward, and Paul Robeson, but she made a young lad from a council estate in Peckham, southeast London, who couldn't sing, read music, or play a musical instrument, feel at ease and as important and interesting as her show business colleagues. In her cosy, comfortable home Elisabeth was animated, down to earth, friendly, and entertaining. Though I couldn't help feeling star struck, I kept it to myself!

After she had signed my copy of her record album *Miss Elisabeth Welch 1933–40*, I prepared to say goodbye, but first I told her that we had a family connection. Elisabeth looked puzzled, but I explained that it was through my

Aunt Esther, who had made dresses for her before the war. To help jog her memory, I showed her a photograph of my aunt, taken just after the war. Elisabeth exclaimed, "Yes, I remember her, the friendly coloured lady with the cockney accent!" On the occasion of my aunt's eightieth birthday, November 29, 1992, Elisabeth kindly sent her a signed photograph.

I did not expect to see Elisabeth again, but I was lucky. The following February I received a call from Andrew Youdell, who worked in the British Film Institute's Regional Film Theatre department. I had organised *Burning an Illusion*, the National Film Theatre's first tribute to the work of black actors in British cinema. Scheduled for June 1983, this was going to feature some of Elisabeth's films, including the two she had made with Paul Robeson in the 1930s. Andrew explained that he had befriended Elisabeth at a party and had organised a private screening for her of the National Film Archive's print of *Song of Freedom*, the first film she had made with Robeson. Would I like to join them? How could I refuse?

On March 4, just a few months after visiting her in Capener's Close, I found myself sitting next to Elisabeth in one of the British Film Institute's tiny and old-fashioned but cosy viewing theatres in Royalty Mews, off Dean Street. Waiting for the curtains to pull back and for the film to start, she leaned over and told me that this was the first time she had seen *Song of Freedom* since its London premiere at the Plaza Cinema in 1936. In fact, the film had rarely surfaced at all in all those years. Elisabeth greeted each appearance of her co-stars with enthusiasm: Connie Smith, Paul Robeson, and Esme Percy were among them. Afterwards she shared anecdotes with us about the making of the film and the actors she had worked with. We thanked Andrew for an enjoyable afternoon, and he promised to invite us back for further private screenings!

Over the next few years Elisabeth and I were occasional guests of Andrew's for lunch at Kettner's Restaurant in Soho, followed by afternoon screenings of films from the National Film Archive. While we lunched at Kettner's it became almost a ritual for Alfredo Ivaldi, the tall, distinguished-looking eighty-year-old singing *maître de* (who had worked at Kettner's for over forty years) to approach Elisabeth. After reminding her that he had seen her in cabaret in Paris in 1930, he serenaded her, much to her delight and the amusement of the customers.

For the screenings that followed lunch, Andrew always consulted Elisabeth about the titles. I enjoyed the choices that she made; these included some of the films in which she had appeared, but Elisabeth also chose musicals or comedies from the "Golden Age" of Hollywood, including *It Happened One Night*, starring Clark Gable and Claudette Colbert; *Top Hat*, starring Fred Astaire and

Ginger Rogers; *To Be or Not to Be,* starring Jack Benny and Carole Lombard; and MGM's *The Band Wagon,* starring Astaire and Jack Buchanan, an old friend of Elisabeth's. We were also treated to several classic "jazz" shorts, including *St. Louis Blues* (1929), starring Bessie Smith, and *Black and Tan Fantasy* (1929), starring Duke Ellington and Fredi Washington, who had been Elisabeth's class mate from Julia Richman High School.

These were memorable, joyous occasions. Each time we met we laughed and laughed, and Elisabeth always had interesting stories to tell us about the stars of the films we viewed. For instance, after the screening of *It Happened One Night* she revealed that in the late 1930s she had befriended the Oscar-winning star of the film, Claudette Colbert, while holidaying in Austria. Andrew and I also organised several film tributes to Elisabeth, including one that involved a trip to Newcastle's Tyneside Cinema in 1984, which was great fun.

Shortly after meeting Elisabeth, I met Derek Jarman. This was during the summer of 1983, when he was in the middle of a seven-year break from feature films. It wasn't his choice. No-one in the British film industry would finance his work, and he hadn't directed any films since *The Tempest* in 1979, in which he had featured Elisabeth. It was a shocking waste of his talent.

Derek described himself as a painter who made films. He was also an eloquent, outspoken campaigner for the rights of gay men. He had heard about my interest in Elisabeth and invited me to his minuscule studio flat in Phoenix House, just off Charing Cross Road, to discuss a project he had in mind. I had never ventured into the world of an artist before. I was quite unprepared for what I encountered.

Derek's flat consisted of a galley kitchen, a tiny bathroom, and a single front room overlooking noisy Charing Cross Road and facing St. Martin's School of Art. Fascinated, I studied the contents, which included a mini-gallery of Jarman's own paintings, some books, and lots of interesting "arty" things. Then something moved under a large duvet [comforter] on a double mattress on the floor. A tousled-haired, naked man, aged about nineteen, stood up; Derek, in his rather quaint, middle-class way, politely asked the lad if he would "go downstairs and have some breakfast." Derek then handed him money "for coffee and a croissant." The young man dressed and left.

Coming from a working-class background, I didn't know what a croissant was, but I didn't embarrass myself by asking Derek to explain. Completely unaware of the world of the artist, I asked Derek where he lived. He looked surprised. "I live here." I continued, "Yes, but when you're not staying in London, surely you must have a big house in the country." Derek laughed, "No. *This* is my only home!"

We talked enthusiastically about Elisabeth, and Derek explained his reason for inviting me. He wanted to make one of his Super-8 home movies about her and, if we could raise the money, possibly transfer it to 16 mm and release it as a forty-minute featurette. He wanted me to put together a proposal and work as a consultant on the project. I agreed that it was a great idea, and I was happy to become involved, but my enthusiasm waned as he explained some of his ideas: "We could film Lis at home in Capener's Close, vacuuming the floor or dusting the piano, while singing 'Stormy Weather.'" Though I smiled and nodded, I secretly found his ideas very stupid and too eccentric for someone as wonderful as Elisabeth. It didn't take long for me to realise that Derek was, as we say in Peckham, "bonkers," but it was exciting to meet him all the same.

A few weeks later Derek arranged for me to meet his "producer," a tall, handsome, well-spoken gentleman called Tim Bevan. He had been trying to raise money for Derek's projects. I liked Tim, and he seemed to appreciate my ideas for a documentary film about Elisabeth, but nothing came of the project, and shortly afterwards Tim made his mark with the critically acclaimed and award-winning *My Beautiful Laundrette* (1985). Since the mid-1980s, as a producer, he has become one of the most influential figures in British cinema, with such titles as *Four Weddings and a Funeral*, *Elizabeth*, *Notting Hill* and *Bridget Jones's Diary* to his credit. Derek found himself back on track in his film career with *Caravaggio* (1986).

I never saw Tim again, but I did correspond, on and off, with Derek for several years, and when I was the film critic for *Gay Times* magazine in the early 1990s, I met him at various press screenings. He was always warm and friendly, even after I wrote a bad review of his 1990 film *The Garden!*

In 1984 Derek kindly invited me to the launch of the publication of his journal *Dancing Ledge*. Elisabeth was the special guest and had been invited to sing a few numbers. These included "Stormy Weather," through a blizzard of confetti, which rained down upon everyone, just as it had done in *The Tempest*. Years later, in 1999, when Tony Peake published his biography of Derek, I was surprised to discover amongst the illustrations a photograph that I had not known existed of Elisabeth singing at the launch. Gazing up at her in adoration from the front row are Derek, the jazz singer George Melly, and me.

Derek was one of the sweetest, most genteel people I have ever met, and, by featuring her in *The Tempest*, he was partly responsible for the renaissance in Elisabeth's career. I'm not sorry he didn't make our film with Elisabeth. A few years after our discussions, David Robinson and Stephen Garrett co-directed a more conventional and appropriate documentary about Elisabeth called *Keeping Love Alive* (1987).

By the mid-1980s Elisabeth's renaissance was well under way, and it was a joy for me to witness, at first hand, this revival in interest of one of the great ladies of British musical theatre. For me, the turning point was her show-stopping appearance at the Donmar Warehouse in *Kern Goes to Hollywood*, an intimate revue that celebrated the songs of Jerome Kern. Critics and audiences "rediscovered" her beauty, magic, and charisma. Critical acclaim, a nomination for a Laurence Olivier award, and guest appearances on television all played parts in returning Elisabeth—in triumph—to her native New York in 1986. It was a "comeback" that earned her a nomination for a Tony award and, in 1989, at the age of eighty-five, an invitation to perform in cabaret at Carnegie Hall.

Though we kept in touch by phone and letter, Elisabeth's full schedule sometimes prevented her from meeting Andrew and me for lunch and screenings. However, I was deeply touched when in the summer of 1988 she found the time, and took the trouble, to send me a kind congratulations card on the occasion of my graduation.

After my graduation, and until her retirement in the mid-1990s, we shared occasional professional associations. In 1989 I organised an "eightieth" birthday tribute to Elisabeth at the Riverside Studios, returning to the venue where I had first met her in 1982. Film extracts were followed by an on-stage interview with David Robinson. In 1992 I persuaded Elisabeth to participate in a BBC documentary called *Black and White in Colour*. I was employed as a researcher on this production, which charted the history of black people in British television. I was also asked to interview some of the contributors. *Black and White in Colour* was directed by the esoteric and intellectual black filmmaker Isaac Julien. On the set, before we began the interview, Elisabeth and I huddled together in a corner and giggled. Our interview over, Isaac kept the camera running and questioned Elisabeth about race. Her reply gave everyone involved in the production a revealing insight into her thoughts on the matter: "I have never separated black and white. It doesn't come into my mind that I'm a black woman doing a show, or a black woman on television. I never put people in blocks. Does that make sense? It comes from my upbringing. I don't look at the colour of a person's face. I just live my life and love the people in my life. I don't choose whether they're black or white."

Finally, in December 1994, I presented a retrospective of Elisabeth's film and television career at the National Film Theatre (see Awards and Tributes, in appendix A). It proved to be a wonderful opportunity to raid the archives and screen a range of titles from the 1930s to the 1990s. Elisabeth happily agreed to participate by taking to the stage for another interview with David Robinson. It was one of her last public appearances.

This book is a personal tribute to one of the great names of British musical theatre, whom I was fortunate to befriend. It is mainly based on interviews and conversations we had during the last twenty or so years of her life, as well as on my collection of memorabilia. I have also drawn from a vast collection of Elisabeth's own memorabilia, which included three scrapbooks, hundreds of press clippings, some private papers, and diaries for every year from 1948 to 1989. These are now in my possession. Other sources of information are acknowledged in the bibliography.

Those seeking here information or revelations from Elisabeth about her private life will be disappointed. Elisabeth was a very private person. She rarely, if ever, spoke about her early marriage to the musician Luke Smith. It was not until 1989 that I first heard her talk about this, in a BBC radio interview with Chris Ellis. Her scrapbooks, diaries, and private papers reveal almost nothing about her personal relationships.

However, I will mention a couple of discoveries I made after she passed away on July 15, 2003. Her friend Derek Granger asked me to search for and select some outstanding critical notices for him to read to the congregation at her funeral service. On many occasions I had sifted through and analysed every scrap of information I had collected or been given about Elisabeth. However, this time I discovered a letter I had not seen before. I was surprised by its existence and its contents. Nothing else in her collection is so personal. I cannot explain why the letter hadn't materialised before. It is a mystery, but I do believe Elisabeth wanted me to discover the letter and read it *after* she had passed away.

The emotionally charged letter is dated October 2, 1944. It was sent to Elisabeth from a hospital in Italy by David Astor, the son of the formidable, flamboyant American-English Tory politician Lady Nancy Astor (1879–1964). In 1919 Lady Astor had become Britain's first woman MP to take her place in the House of Commons. Unlike his mother, David Astor was a Liberal. He was the editor of the *Observer* newspaper from 1948 to 1975. At the time he wrote the letter he was convalescing from a wound received while serving his country. In addition to expressing his feelings for Elisabeth, Astor mourns the recent execution—on August 26, 1944—of his close friend Adam von Trott, who had been involved in an assassination attempt on Adolf Hitler.

The Astor estate refused permission for me to publish the letter in this book. However, other letters I had already found in the collection dating from the 1980s, as well as several entries in her diary, confirm that in 1985 Elisabeth and David renewed their friendship after meeting at a concert. On March 4, 1987, for his seventy-fifth birthday celebration at the Waldorf Hotel, Elisabeth accepted an invitation to attend and sing to David and his guests. He passed away in London on December 7, 2001, at the age of eighty-nine.

Then there is "Pepe." Numerous meetings and telephone calls with Pepe are mentioned in Elisabeth's diaries from 1948 to 1988, but the gentleman is not identified. There is no mention of him in several surviving address books. The name meant nothing to me until a year after Elisabeth had passed away and some memorabilia, once belonging to Elisabeth, was given to me. Searching through the photographs and letters, I discovered a small batch of fading press clippings about Jose de Togores, Marquis of Santa Cruz.

Through the years I had heard rumours about a close friendship Elisabeth had had with a "Spanish ambassador," but I had made no enquiries. One of the press clippings revealed that the Marquis of Santa Cruz had been the Spanish ambassador to the Court of St. James's in London from 1958 to 1972; it described him as "dark, friendly, supremely courteous and widely known to his friends as Pepe."

A grandson of the Spanish minister to Britain in 1866, "Pepe" was born in Madrid in 1902, partly educated at Oxford, and entered the diplomatic service in 1921. He was originally based in London from 1933 to 1948 and was then sent to work as a minister in Copenhagen. Elisabeth's passports confirm that she made a number of visits to Copenhagen from 1948 until Pepe's return to London in 1958. Pepe and Elisabeth remained in regular contact, either in person or by telephone, almost until he passed away in Madrid on June 15, 1988, at the age of eighty-six. He made a telephone call to her on Christmas Day, 1986, and one further—final—call on New Year's Day, 1988. I believe that the press clippings about Pepe came into my possession for a reason, for they materialised just a week before I was due to send this manuscript to the publisher, just giving me time to mention them in this book.

CHAPTER ONE

Girlie

Girlie's on the boards, she's doomed!

Elisabeth always kept her age a secret. It remained a mystery to everyone. However, in the information she originally provided for two 1930s editions of Pitman's *Who's Who in the Theatre*, she gave the correct year of her birth. In the eighth (1936) and ninth (1939) editions she gave 1904, but in the tenth (1947) edition she changed it to 1908, and this remained the case until the final sixteenth (1977) edition, when she altered it to 1909. Interestingly, her passports were consistent. From the 1930s to the 1990s she always stated 1909!

Attempts by the author to trace a copy of her birth certificate in New York failed, partly because of the uncertainty of the year of her birth, partly because it was not known that Elisabeth had altered the spelling of her surname.

Shortly after her death her friend, the BBC radio producer Michael Alexander confirmed what many had only speculated about. Some years earlier he had located a copy of her birth certificate, but out of respect to Elisabeth, and to avoid upsetting her, he had kept the information private. A copy was also located by a New York fan, Professor Edward Mapp. The certificate confirmed that she had been registered as Elisabeth Margaret Welsh. Her date of birth was recorded as February 27, 1904. However, the place of birth differed from the one Elisabeth had given. She claimed that she had been born in New York City on West 63d Street, but her birthplace was recorded as 223 West 61st Street.

The certificate confirmed that her father was John Wesley Welsh, age thirty-five years, of Delaware, Maryland, and that her mother was Elisabeth Kay, thirty-two, of Scotland. However, this information does not correspond with Elisabeth's claim that her father had been at least twenty years older than her mother. Also, in her 1971 diary she recorded her mother's date of birth as March 23, 1877, which suggests that her mother was actually twenty-six at the time of Elisabeth's birth.

With reference to Elisabeth's surname, Michael Alexander explained that when he presented her with the copy of her birth certificate, she informed him that she had hated the name Welsh and changed it to Welch in the late 1920s. On the cast lists of her early Broadway shows, including *Runnin' Wild* (1923) and *Blackbirds of 1928*, her surname is given as Welsh. Thereafter her professional surname became Welch. Though she objected to the *s* in Welsh, she insisted on keeping the *s* in Elisabeth, as she explained to the London *Evening News* in September 1933: "I don't like 'z' and if I used it in my name it would change my life entirely. Names are very important. I believe in numerology. I don't bet very often, but once I tried numerology at a race meeting and won every time. It may sound an exaggeration, but it's true."

Elisabeth was always clear about her mixed-race ancestry—African, Native American, Scots, and Irish—but she was not forthcoming about her ancestors: "Our father told us about his family. Unfortunately we never wrote it down. We never thought that we should." She did recall a photograph that existed "on tin" of her father's mother, a Native American of the Lenape tribe of Wilmington, on the Delaware River in Maryland. She was also told that her paternal grandfather had come to America from Africa on a slave ship and that Welsh was the surname of his owner. Her grandmother was run off the reservation for marrying an African.

John Welsh worked as a gardener, coachman, and general factotum on a large private estate belonging to a millionaire in Englewood, New Jersey. He only came home on weekends. Elisabeth Kay, the daughter of a longshoreman who played the fiddle, had been born in Leith, which used to be a large port in its own right but had become part of Edinburgh. She was mostly Scottish, but with an Irish grandmother with the surname Milligan. Put into service when she was sixteen, Elisabeth was brought to America to work as an assistant to the nanny of the same Englewood family that employed John Welsh:

> That's how they met but nobody would marry them. Mama told me about the difficulty they had in getting somebody to marry them because mixed marriages were illegal. They finally found a Catholic priest who married them in

secret. My mother was a wonderful woman. She was brave and defiant. She adored me and my two brothers, Edward and John, and we adored her. It must have been awful for her, this tall white lady with three brown children around her, coming home from school, with people staring at her and wondering who the hell she was but she was a defiant woman. It was only when we were all grown up that we learned to appreciate what she had done for us and how much she had fought for us.

Elisabeth was born in a blizzard ("which is perhaps why I like the snow so much!") and confirmed in the Cathedral of St. John the Divine in New York, one of the most beautiful church buildings in the United States. She lived with her family in a mixed neighbourhood that she described as West 63d Street between Columbus Avenue and Tenth Avenue, close to where the Lincoln Centre is, and where the Metropolitan Opera House stands:

It used to be called San Juan Hill. It was close to Central Park, my playground. We were poor, of course, but we didn't want for anything. It was a bit rough but I loved it. There were Irish, who were cops as well, Italians, who were Mafia as well, a German butcher and a Swiss delicatessen. It was a bit like London's Soho. We would go to Irish wakes hoping for the cold ham and sandwiches. Of course we had to be careful on St. Patrick's Day because the Irish tried to beat us up. So Mama, who was a Scot and very white, used to keep us indoors. She wouldn't take us to school but I never had any feeling about being different from anybody else. I was never confined to a physical or mental ghetto. It equipped me to be an international person all my life.

Throughout her life, Elisabeth was a night owl, and friends knew better than to call her before lunchtime. Some put this down to her life in the theatre and its unsocial hours, but Elisabeth explained that it had nothing to do with this: "I have never gone to bed early. It has nothing to with my being in the theatre. As a child Mama couldn't get me to bed and she couldn't get me up in the morning. Many times Mama had to dip a facecloth in cold water to put over my face to get me to school. I love the night. I live at night. I can go to bed at six o'clock in the evening but I don't put my light out until four or five in the morning. I read or watch television."

The Welsh family lived in a tenement block. When Elisabeth was five years old there was a fire in the apartment below. Mama Welsh grabbed baby John and headed for the fire escape with Elisabeth racing on ahead, but when they got to the roof there was no sign of Elisabeth. Her mother couldn't believe her eyes when she saw her young daughter waving to her from the roof of the adjoining block. In 1985 brother John recalled in British television's

This Is Your Life tribute: "I think the whole of New York must have heard Mama shouting, 'don't jump!' because it seemed Elisabeth was going to jump back over. They had those old tenement houses in those days separated by air shafts and Elisabeth in her frenzy leaped from our side of the roof over the shaft to the adjoining building. This was about four feet. Our mother almost fainted."

To avoid confusion about their names, Elisabeth's father called his wife Liz or Lizzie, which neither mother nor daughter liked: "So I was called Girlie to make it easier." Elisabeth, brought up between two brothers, Eddie (born August 30, 1902) and John (born September 27, 1906), admitted she was a tomboy: "I used to play basketball with them and row in Central Park. I was horrid really. I didn't like girls. I didn't dislike them, but I liked boys better. I wasn't a dainty little thing, except that Mama did send me to dancing school, but I was always the boy. I did the leading! My mother asked, 'Where are your girlfriends?' because I was always bringing boys back to our home."

Elisabeth would claim that there was music throughout her whole family: "We all sang, because we loved singing. My elder brother had a beautiful bass, and my younger brother had a light baritone. My mother sang also, but she always wanted to play the piano. She never got the chance, however. My father sang a bit, too, and he had a brother who played the trombone. So a piano was bought when we were children and we all had lessons. My elder brother and I gave it up, finally, but my younger brother carried through and went on to study in Berlin."

One of the first songs to make an impression on Elisabeth made *quite* an impression! At the age of eight, Elisabeth visited her next door neighbour, who had a Pianola roll, and later claimed she learned a lot of songs from it: "One particular song took my fancy, and I learned the words and melody. I whistled, sung, and hummed it. So one day my mother heard me singing it and said 'Girlie, what's that song you're singing?' So I sang it for her. Well, she gave me such a smack, that I went spinning around the table and I was absolutely livid. The song was 'When I Get You Alone Tonight.'"

As a youngster, Elisabeth attended Public School 59. Later, at Julia Richman High School, for girls only, her "international" outlook was also influenced by the "pals" she made. They included a Jewish girl, Millie Hoffman or Hoffmanstahl; an Italian, Teresa Savarini; a German, Elsie Loffler; "and another was a coloured girl, Arsine Becaud, who was half-French." At Julia Richman, Elisabeth also befriended Fredi Washington and her older sister Isabel. Fredi went on the stage about the same time as Elisabeth and appeared in such important films as *Black and Tan Fantasy* (1929), with Duke Ellington, and *Imitation of Life* (1934), in which she portrayed the light-skinned

Peola Johnson, who passes for white. She was also Paul Robeson's leading lady in the film version of Eugene O'Neill's *The Emperor Jones* (1933), three years before Elisabeth co-starred with Robeson. Isabel, who also had a theatrical career, was featured with the blues singer Bessie Smith in the latter's only film, *St. Louis Blues* (1929). As far as Elisabeth was concerned, her "pals" were the same as her. They were all New Yorkers, and she didn't think about the colour of their skin or their race: "I never felt that I had to fight anything. My closest friends at school were a German and a Swede and they lived around the corner because it was a mixed neighbourhood. I wasn't particularly clever at school. I lived in the gymnasium."

Elisabeth was destined to go on the stage:

> I realised later that I was born to be on the stage because as a youngster I *acted* as though I were! I had my first experience of the theatre when Mama took me to hear a performance of Gilbert and Sullivan at the Century Theater in Central Park West and my first stage appearance was in Gilbert and Sullivan's *H.M.S. Pinafore* with the Choral Society. There was a famous theatre we used to go to called the Colonial Theater on Columbus Circle, near to where we lived on 63rd Street. It used to have variety shows. Then there was the Lincoln Square Cinema where they had variety acts between the main films. I used to go to the shows with my older brother Eddie on Saturday mornings for a nickel [five cents]. During the summer months the performers sat on the fire escapes to keep cool, and I would stare at them whenever I passed. I was always fascinated by their make-up.

John Welsh was a strict Baptist, but Elisabeth and her mother were Episcopalians:

> We belonged to St. Cyprians, an Episcopalian church, and we had a settlement in the parish hall. This was a meeting place for mothers and children and I helped out at all kinds of functions. I sang at the concerts they gave there, organised church bazaars, and ran clubs for boys and girls. I taught them to dance the Scottish reel and Irish jig. I staged little shows with kids aged from about four to eight years old. I almost killed one little girl in the middle of a fierce winter. We had snow piled up in the streets. I put on a Christmas show and I made her the New Year's Angel. She had a little diaper on, a gold crown on her head and some wings, and she got pneumonia. That was the first time I started praying. I prayed and prayed every night, "Oh, Lord, save her." Adele was her name and, thank goodness, she pulled through. So my ambition was to be a social worker but of course I always sang. I began singing when I was seven years old in the Sunday School choir and at the age of thirteen I graduated to the church choir.

Elisabeth was always proud that she sang with the church choir in St. John's Cathedral in New York, where she had been confirmed, but during choir practice Elisabeth started drinking: "I was born under Pisces and all Pisceans like a drink. I used to steal the communion wine and take a nip. I think that's why I've never been a drunk because I've been at it too long! I worried about going to Hell because of it, but now I just think, well, I'll meet all my friends there." In those days Elisabeth was called "the loud alto," because she had a strong voice and always sang in key. She also laughed too much: "I was always getting into trouble for laughing. I laughed through weddings and funerals." Elisabeth credited the organist at St. Cyprians for her musical training. The organist told the choir, "We can hear the music but words have been written and they tell a story so we want to hear the words because you're singing a story."

Elisabeth made her brothers laugh when she started sucking lemons: "I thought all divas, all the grand opera singers, sucked lemons. I don't know where I got that from. I must have heard it because it does tighten your throat. So I started practising being a diva from an early age!"

On West 63d Street, opposite St. Cyprians, there was the Music Hall where Mae West created a sensation with her all-boys show:

> Mae West kept that show running for years! The men were in drag and in those days we just thought 'Well, that's theatre!' The Music Hall was next to a fire station and a police station, and the police used to raid the place more or less every Saturday night. They'd wait for the show to finish the week—that's how crooked it was—and then, just after the performers did their finale on Saturday night, clang-clang-clang would come the Black Marias. The police led Mae and the boys out of the theatre and they were still in their dressing gowns. To defy them, the boys swished out wearing long eye-lashes and lipstick, *mincing* out of the theatre and into the police wagons! Now, this was just after the First World War so it was frightfully shocking behaviour for most people to see. We had Saturday choir practice every week at St. Cyprians, so we'd stand on the church stairs across the street and watch all this going on, laughing our heads off, and all the firemen would be laughing too! So, Mae West was the first great person of the theatre that I saw—but not on stage! Years later I met her in London. She was not brash, like she was in her films, but so gentle you could hardly hear her talk. I admired the enormous topaz jewels she was wearing: matching necklace, earrings, bracelet and ring. Miss West explained seriously that this was merely her "summer jewellery." I wanted to laugh, but she was so sweet that I couldn't.

Elisabeth made her Broadway stage debut, billed on the cast list as a "Brown Skin Vamp," in Irving C. Miller's tuneful and popular *Liza* at Daly's Theatre on November 27, 1922. However, she did not consider *Liza*—or her next stage appearance as Ruth Little in Flournoy Miller and Aubrey Lyles's *Runnin' Wild*—as "professional," because she was still a member of the church choir. The choir was occasionally hired for concerts; the head of the choir was asked to take them into *Liza* and *Runnin' Wild*, which opened at the Colonial Theatre, a former vaudeville house, on October 29, 1923. Critics praised the show, and some claimed that it was the equal of Noble Sissle and Eubie Blake's 1921 hit *Shuffle Along* (see chapter 2). James P. Johnson and Cecil Mack's songs received considerable praise; these included the rhythmic "Charleston," which seemed to capture the spirit of the Roaring Twenties. Elisabeth said she was chosen to sing the "Charleston" because she had a loud voice:

This was the song that launched the famous dance craze but I thought the lyrics were awful. I sang the verse and chorus, made a quick exit, and the chorus girls, who looked marvellous in their lovely costumes, came forward and danced it. I had to work my way to the side of the stage and get off quick. If I didn't dash off I'd be thrown into the orchestra pit! That song has followed me through my life. Whenever I hear the "Charleston" I think, "Oh, God, I sang that first." I've never danced in my life, which is the crazy thing, because I adore tap dancing. I'm coming back in the next world as Eleanor Powell!

An unidentified theatre critic for the *New York Herald* (October 30, 1923) noted, "Sprightly Elizabeth [*sic*] Welsh stopped the show with a Charleston number in which the phenomenally agile chorus agitated around like a syncopated waterfall."

In 1930 James Weldon Johnson, the celebrated African American writer—and a leading figure in the Harlem Renaissance—acknowledged the importance of the "Charleston" in *Black Manhattan*, his acclaimed history of African Americans in New York:

Runnin' Wild would have been notable if for no other reason than that it made use of the Charleston, a Negro dance creation which up to that time had been known only to Negroes; thereby introducing it to New York, America, and the world. The music for the dance was written by Jimmie Johnson, the composer of the musical score of the piece. The Charleston achieved a popularity second only to the tango. . . . There is a claim that Irving C. Miller first introduced the Charleston on the stage in his *Liza*; even so, it was *Runnin' Wild* that started the dance on its world-encircling course. When Miller and Lyles introduced the dance in their show, they did not depend wholly upon their extraordinarily good jazz band for the accompaniment; they went straight back to primitive Negro music and the major part of the chorus supplement the band by beating out the time with hand-clapping and foot-patting. The effect was electrical. Such a demonstration of beating out complex rhythms had never before been seen on a stage in New York.

Elisabeth was also given her first speaking role in the theatre in *Runnin' Wild*: "I was picked out by Miller and Lyles, two *black* black-face comedians, to play the ghost in a sketch set in a graveyard. Draped in grey cheesecloth I delivered my line from behind a tombstone, 'Whoooooo!'"

Just before Elisabeth left home to make her first appearance in *Runnin' Wild*, her mother threw an old shoe down the stairs at her, for good luck. It was an old superstition, but her father's reaction was more dramatic:

He disapproved. He was a strict Baptist and very old-fashioned. He said, "whistling girls and crowing hens, never come to good ends." He was happy for me to sing in the church choir, and approved of my first stage appearance at the age of eight in an amateur production of H.M.S. *Pinafore* since he liked Gilbert and Sullivan but we had to keep it a secret that I was appearing in real stage shows outside school hours. When he discovered I was appearing in *Runnin' Wild* he more or less blamed Mama, and said that she'd been helping me to do it, which of course she wasn't. He associated show business with low life and he thought I would become a whore, a streetwalker. It was very sad because he said to me one day "I don't like what you're doing" and took a poker to me. Mama thought he might kill me, so I left home for a while, and stayed with friends. Father adored me. I was the apple of his eye, being the only daughter, and he felt betrayed. Shortly afterwards he washed his hands of the family. His parting words were, "Girlie's on the boards, she's doomed." He turned to hate me, and that was terrible. Then he disappeared. He never came home. We never saw him again. It was a blow because we loved him very much. It was a terrible thing, because Mama was terribly upset. She grieved and I felt rotten. We tried to trace him but he'd left his work on the Englewood estate and drew out some money he had in the bank. So we were left and I had to look after my mother, which I loved doing. I continued working in the theatre to help my mother, though I always returned to the church settlement and my work in the community.

CHAPTER TWO

~

The Jazz Age

Not a Harlem Girl

In the Jazz Age, Elisabeth may have helped to introduce its signature tune, the "Charleston," but she had nothing to do with jazz or the Harlem Renaissance as such. This lady did not sing the blues or work at the Cotton Club, or in Harlem at all:

> I'm not a Harlem girl. I'm 63d Street! My mother, being Scottish and an Episcopalian, wouldn't allow Bessie Smith's records in the house. I never saw Ma Rainey. She was before my time. I wasn't a blues girl. I was more Scots than anything else. I was more likely to sing "Keep Right on to the End of the Road" than "St. Louis Blues"!

When Elisabeth was in her twenties, during the Prohibition era, her brother Eddie took her to a Harlem speakeasy, and that was her introduction to the "jazz age":

> Later on we went to the smart place, the Cotton Club, up in Harlem, to hear Cab Calloway. Eddie gave me my first drink at the Club. It was port. "You have this for communion anyhow," he said. The smart whites were in the audience and occasionally they accepted light-skinned Negroes. That's why Eddie and I were allowed in. The Club was run by gangsters. The chorus girls were so beautiful, what we called "high yellow" then. You had to be very pale to work in the Cotton Club. Some of the girls were blonde, genuine blonde, and with blue or grey eyes. The comedians and the male dancers could be dark-skinned but not the girls.

9

Raised in the Episcopal church, Elisabeth had been a Sunday school teacher from the age of twelve, and she continued teaching kindergarten children right into the 1920s, even after helping to launch the "Charleston" in *Runnin' Wild*. Elisabeth fully intended to continue her career as a kindergarten teacher, and from 1924 to 1928 she was employed as a child welfare worker with a branch of the Henry Street Settlement in New York City, but occasionally she found herself sidetracked into Broadway shows.

Before she appeared in *Liza* and *Runnin' Wild*, Elisabeth attended a performance of Noble Sissle and Eubie Blake's Broadway musical *Shuffle Along*, which featured an African American cast. Opening at the 63d Street Music Hall on May 23, 1921, *Shuffle Along* is frequently cited as marking the beginning of the Harlem Renaissance, as writer Langston Hughes explained in *The Big Sea* (1940): "The 1920s were the years of Manhattan's black Renaissance. . . . It was the musical revue, *Shuffle Along*, that gave a scintillating send-off to that Negro vogue in Manhattan, which reached its peak just before the crash of 1929. . . . It gave just the proper push—a pre-Charleston kick—to that Negro vogue of the '20s, that spread to books, African sculpture, music and dancing." Adelaide Hall began her glittering career in *Shuffle Along*, and during the run its star, Gertrude Saunders, was succeeded by Florence Mills. Paul Robeson appeared briefly in a singing quartet, and in August 1922 Josephine Baker joined the road company as a chorus girl. Hall, Mills, Robeson, and Baker were all to have impacts on Elisabeth.

After leaving the cast of *Shuffle Along*, Florence Mills went on to become one of the most popular entertainers of her generation. Famed in New York and London, she was the original star of Lew Leslie's *Blackbirds* revue and introduced such memorable songs as "I'm a Little Blackbird Looking for a Bluebird" and "Silver Rose." Elisabeth adored Florence and kept a small, signed photograph of the star:

I was a kid and still living on 63d Street when *Shuffle Along* opened at the 63rd Street Music Hall. It was a lovely, little intimate theatre and it was right across from my church, St. Cyprians. I rushed to see it. Florence Mills had a joyful smile. She wasn't a noisy person at all. She was very gentle and had a nice, kind face. We adored her without even knowing her, and that was her strength on the stage as well. It came over. She was sweet and everybody loved her, especially when she sang "I'm a Little Blackbird Looking for a Bluebird." That was cute. Florence was meek and mild, a gentle child. She didn't have a big voice, but she could sing and put over songs. She was shy and didn't go to theatre parties. She went home every night with her husband, Ulysses S. Thompson, who was also on the stage. He was a very nice man, a tap dancer. We didn't know what the "S" stood for, so we called him United States Thompson! There was no truth in the rumour that, when she was starring in *Blackbirds* in London, she had an affair with the Prince of Wales [later known as King Edward VIII and then the Duke of Windsor]. Florence wouldn't have had an affair with anybody but Ulysses. There wasn't a sign of theatre about her, no sign at all. She wasn't flamboyant in dress, character, or in her humour. We were noisy in those days but she was a gentle creature.

At the turn of the century, black stage performers like Bert Williams, who starred in *In Dahomey* and then appeared in some of the famous Ziegfeld shows, had to put on blackface. Elisabeth acknowledged that it was Williams and his contemporaries who "pushed open the doors" for 1920s artistes like Florence Mills and Paul Robeson, who were among the first generation to appear on stage without blackface make-up. Sadly, Florence Mills died in 1927 at the age of thirty-one, without ever having made a record. Six years later, by way of a tribute, Elisabeth recorded Florence's "Silver Rose" in London:

She had an appendicitis that burst and she was gone. That was very common in those days. A lot of people died from a burst appendix. They should not have rushed her back to New York from London because if they had attended her here, she could have been saved. Florence's death was a shock to everybody. Her funeral in New York was a show star's funeral because they started the procession down at the riverhead and the cortege came up Fifth Avenue or Madison Avenue. All the time the drums beat at that slow funeral pace and the streets were jammed from the Bowery right up to Harlem. She was treated with great respect. She was so gentle and adored by everybody, and there are very few people you can say that about in our profession.

In Noble Sissle and Eubie Blake's *The Chocolate Dandies* Elisabeth joined a cast that included Josephine Baker. The show had extensive tours that lasted a total of sixty weeks before opening at the Colonial Theatre on September 1, 1924. Elisabeth was featured as Jessie Johnson and had one song to perform, "That Charleston Dance." Baker, two years younger than Elisabeth, was less than a year away from travelling to France to star in *La Revue Negre*, which launched her in Paris and helped transform her into a legend. In 1988, in her foreword to Bryan Hammond and Patrick O'Connor's *Josephine Baker* (see bibliography), Elisabeth remembered her first encounter with Baker. In the unedited version, found amongst her papers, she said:

She glowed. She had glamour. She wanted admiration. "Look at me! Look at me!" That is how I shall always remember Josephine Baker. We were in the same show. We were about the same age. She was a lead—I was a beginner. Meeting her going in or out of the stage-door, I noticed how tall she walked.

Her head held high—and swathed in a bright piece of silk—she looked like an Eastern princess. To complete the picture, she wore a black sealskin coat, trimmed in red fox, which she lovingly held against her body like a show-girl displaying her beauty. "Look at me!" Then off she went to Paris.

Even though they both became expatriates, Elisabeth did not feel a particular kinship with Baker: "We didn't think like that in those days. She was a dancer, a beautiful woman with a body that any sculptor would glorify, and she was an enormous success."

Lew Leslie had been planning to star Florence Mills in his next edition of *Blackbirds* on Broadway. After she died on November 1, 1927, Leslie reorganised the show, with singers Adelaide Hall and Aida Ward taking the leads. The tap dancer Bill "Bojangles" Robinson was hired during the out-of-town tryout. Meanwhile, choirmaster Cecil Mack (Richard C. McPherson), who had provided the lyric for "Charleston" in *Runnin' Wild* (see chapter 1), heard Elisabeth singing in the choir at St. Cyprian's. At his invitation, she joined Cecil Mack's Choir, and in 1928 she found herself with the choir in the cast of Leslie's new revue, *Blackbirds of 1928*, which opened at the Liberty Theatre on May 9, 1928, and ran for 518 performances. A knockout score by Jimmy McHugh (music) and Dorothy Fields (lyrics) included "I Can't Give You Anything But Love," "Doin' the New Low-Down," and "Porgy." With such talent involved, it couldn't help become the most successful *Blackbirds* production and the longest-running all-black cast revue in Broadway history.

Elisabeth was proud of her association with *Blackbirds of 1928* and always maintained that it was her *professional* stage debut: "I was quite happy singing in Cecil Mack's Choir. On Sundays I continued singing in my own church choir at St. Cyprian's but a few months into the run of *Blackbirds* they heard this 'loud alto' in the choir and gave me some understudy work to do."

At the same time *Blackbirds* was running, there was a play on Broadway called *Porgy*. Written by Du Bose Heyward, it was the story and book from which George Gershwin later based his folk opera *Porgy and Bess*. A song had been written by Fields and McHugh in which Aida Ward described one of the scenes in *Porgy*. She came onto the stage as Bess, in her red dress, and sang about her love for Porgy. Elisabeth, as a member of Cecil Mack's Choir, participated in the scene and was chosen to understudy Ward. In the star's absence she went on and sang "Porgy" three times. Elisabeth remained fond of the song. Nearly sixty years later, in 1987, she sang it in the documentary film *Keeping Love Alive* (see chapter 10).

Bill Robinson was a great success with his appearance in the second act, performing "Doin' the New Low-Down." Audiences loved him, and he went on to Hollywood stardom in four Shirley Temple films, but off-stage he was unpopular. Lena Horne, who later co-starred with Robinson in the Hollywood musical *Stormy Weather*, described him as the biggest Uncle Tom in show biz: "He carried a revolver, was poisonous to other blacks, and truly believed in the wit and wisdom of Shirley Temple." Elisabeth remembered him as a "difficult man," but also one who "loved to be loved":

> Some people didn't warm to him. Bill was the sort of person who expected you to run up to him and kiss him, and I hadn't got to that part of my life where I could do that to someone, unless it was a close friend. I was rather detached from everything and everyone at that time, and not as relaxed as I became later on. I don't believe in pushing myself. I love cats and dogs, but I wait for them to come to me. Bill liked me and he pushed me into making my first record. It was "Doin' the New Low-Down," the song he made famous in *Blackbirds*.

Elisabeth recorded "Doin' the New Low-Down" and "Diga Diga Doo," by Fields and McHugh, with Irving Mills and His Hotsy-Totsy Gang, in New York on July 27, 1928.

In *Blackbirds of 1928*, "Diga Diga Doo" was introduced by Adelaide Hall and a chorus of beautiful girls in red sequins in a pseudo-African jungle setting. Hall later recalled, "I hardly wore anything at all, just beads and feathers. It upset my family very much. Especially my mother! Some people have complained that the lyrics to the song are offensive, but at the time I didn't see anything wrong with it. I was young and enjoying the excitement of being part of a successful Broadway show." Elisabeth had nothing but praise for Hall's performance: "She was fantastic in that number! The audience just roared their approval." Adelaide later described what Elisabeth was like during the run of *Blackbirds*: "She kept herself to herself and didn't mix with the rest of us. After the show she went straight home to her mother, whom she adored."

Though Elisabeth (from 1933) and Adelaide (from 1939) became long-term London residents and remained friendly, they never socialised and hardly ever performed together. In 1980 they returned to New York to appear in the revue *Black Broadway* (see chapter 10) with other great names of the black Broadway shows of the 1920s. Regrettably, they were never invited to appear on television or record an album as a duo. However, there were two impromptu appearances in London in the early 1980s when they attended performances by visiting African Americans. On December 23, 1981, they attended a performance of *Snowshoe Shuffle* at London's Riverside Studios. This featured some of the great African American tap dancers, including

Honi Coles, Chuck Green, and Will Gaines. During the show, Elisabeth and Adelaide were persuaded to come to the stage and sing a duet, "Bye Bye Blackbird." When the jazz musician Benny Carter was in London in 1984, Elisabeth and Adelaide were in the audience one night (November 28) whilst he was performing at the Pizza Express in Dean Street. More than a little magic was conjured up when both ladies were persuaded to join Carter on stage. That evening Elisabeth performed "Poor Butterfly," one of the songs she had recorded with Carter in London in 1936 (see chapter 5).

On television in 1985 Adelaide made a guest appearance in Elisabeth's *This Is Your Life* tribute, and in 1991 they took part in the *Cole Porter Centennial Gala* at the Prince Edward Theatre in London. Adelaide sang "What Is This Thing Called Love?" and Elisabeth sang "Love for Sale." Adelaide died at the age of ninety-two on November 7, 1993; in 1994 Elisabeth attended her memorial service at St. Paul's, known as the "actor's church," in London's Covent Garden.

Elisabeth rarely spoke about her brief marriage to the trumpet player Luke Smith, Jr., Born in Ripley, Ohio, in the 1890s, he was the son of Luke Smith, Sr., and had six brothers, all of them trumpet players, including the most famous, Russell T. Smith. Another brother, Joe Smith, was the favourite accompanist of the blues singer Bessie Smith (no relation). Luke Junior had been a member of the pit band for *The Chocolate Dandies* in 1924. When he replaced Elmer Chambers in Fletcher Henderson's orchestra for a short while in December 1925, the line-up for Henderson's trumpet section included Luke and his two brothers, Russell and Joe. Elisabeth would confirm that she married Luke on her birthday, February 27, 1928, just before she joined the cast of *Blackbirds of 1928*. She wanted to get away from home: "My family and friends didn't want me to do it and proved they were right." The couple lived in a seven-room apartment with Joe. However, Luke was unhappy with his wife's stage career and tried to persuade her to quit *Blackbirds*. Elisabeth said the marriage only lasted for one year, ending "when I left New York to go to Paris with *Blackbirds* for an engagement at the Moulin Rouge" (see chapter 3). Luke Matthew Smith, Jr., died suddenly at the Rhythm Club in New York in 1936. Legend has it that he carried a torch for Elisabeth to the end and died of a broken heart.

At the end of the decade, Elisabeth met Ethel Waters, a great African American star of the Harlem Renaissance: "I knew her name when I was a kid because she was a big name and a great artist. In the 1920s, when I lived in 128th Street in New York City, she lived in the bad part of Harlem, on 5th Avenue, a rather poor area. She had a reputation as a tough lady. She sang in nightclubs, not the nightclubs we knew with white tablecloths, but dives and cellars, where you took your own bottle of drink. She had great respect as an artist but she didn't sing in smart places." In the 1920s Waters lived in Harlem with her girlfriend Ethel Williams: "They were known as 'The Two Ethels' but I was very young and didn't know about lesbians. It was scandalous for two women to live together. This other Ethel was skinny, and red-haired. She had no personality at all. Ethel Waters was called a bull dyke, a terrible name." Elisabeth met Waters in Paris in 1929:

She was adorable, a lovely, charming person. Gentle, quiet and nice. She was a marvellous singer, had a lovely face and she had fun. She didn't like everybody, especially girl singers. After I met her she gave Billie Holiday and Lena Horne a hard time, but fortunately she liked me, even though I was a singer. I found her an ordinary person, not educated, and somewhat shy. I think she wanted to be friendly but didn't know how. I saw her again in New York after the war. It must have been about 1946. She sang in her bedroom slippers. In her younger days Ethel Waters was thin and quite attractive. She only got heavy later on when she became religious and her eye was on the sparrow! After she became famous, Ethel turned the other way, but her relationships with men were disastrous. They abused and exploited her. Eventually she turned her back on men, took up religion, and preached the word of God till the day she died. It's so sad she ended up with that man Billy Graham, the evangelist, singing hymns, gathering flock for Jesus. In doing so, I felt she lost her sense of humour, and became a sad person.

Finding herself in Paris at the age of twenty-five, Elisabeth was destined, it seems, to travel from an early age. When she was a very small girl in New York she was occasionally taken, as a treat, to stay at her God-mother's house for a night; it was after one of these visits that she remembered her Mama saying, "You'll be a traveller, I can see that. You sleep so happily in strange beds."

I think my mother made that observation entirely from her own experience, for she had the travel-bug, having left Edinburgh to sail for America and a new life at such a young age. So the travel-bug I inherited from my mother's side. It was hearing her stories of Scotland and her childhood that first fired my imagination to one day see the land of Mama's birth.

CHAPTER THREE

~

Paris

First Class with a Third Class fare

Elisabeth arrived in Paris with the *Blackbirds* company, without Bill Robinson, in May 1929. When the show opened at the Moulin Rouge on June 7, it was a sensation. Some of France's top stars attended, including Mistinguett, Maurice Chevalier, Grock, Jean Gabin, and Barbette. Without Robinson, Adelaide Hall became the star attraction, and the French critics loved her, describing her as a rival to Josephine Baker. Elisabeth loved Paris:

My days in Paris were absolutely splendid. Marvellous. When I got to Paris the atmosphere was completely relaxed, compared to America. I was more or less tied to the Montmarte section and that's where I got to know the French, especially the cabaret set. I never had any trouble because the French loved to have a mixture of peoples and cabaret was a mixture of peoples. The French were nice and polite to us because they knew we were show people. There was another coloured girl who came over with *Blackbirds*, her name was Henrietta, and we became pals. She wanted to go to the bars because they let women into the bars in Montmarte and all over Paris for that matter, but only if you were decent and dressed nicely. We weren't picking up men so we were allowed to go into the bars which were open all night. Everybody was pleasant and happy. Then you got your taxi and went home at two or three or four in the morning. Henrietta and I got to know the ladies of the night and they told us their stories. Many of them sold cocaine, then very chic with the smart set. They sold it cut price, and not only the price. They mixed it with cheap talcum powder or Epsom salts to make it glimmer. Then we'd go to a restaurant and people

17

would recognise us—"Oh, you're from *Blackbirds*. Would you sing for us?" So we would sing a song, and we got to know a lot of people that way. That's how I got to know a divine man called Louis Moyses who owned two popular night-clubs, Le Boeuf sur le Toit and Le Grand Écart. He was adorable. He said "Elis-abeth, if you ever want a job you must come to your grandmama." He called himself my grandmama. It was a marvellous time.

In 1922 Moyses, a bartender from Charlesville, created Le Boeuf in Rue Boissy-d'Anglas off the Place de la Concorde. Throughout the 1920s, Le Boeuf prospered as a lively meeting place for everyone in the artistic move-ment, mostly writers and designers. It did, in fact, outlast the many restau-rants and bars that made Paris so fashionable in the Jazz Age. Le Boeuf had been designed by Jean Cocteau. Elisabeth described it as "very *moderne*, very chic, all steel and black. Cocteau designed a marble entrance and he had this bull on the roof." In September 1929 Elisabeth returned to New York with the *Blackbirds* company: "My return to New York coincided with the famous Wall Street crash, and there was no work. So I wrote to Moyses, and he sent me a ticket. I went back to Paris in late January 1930 and Moyses gave me a job at Le Boeuf and found me an apartment."

Moyses gave Elisabeth a spot during the cocktail hour, which was from six thirty to eight, but she soon graduated to the dinner hour. This is where the transformation from being the "loud alto" in her church choir to sophisti-cated cabaret singer took place: "I have never arranged anything in my life. I have no push myself, but once I get the thing to do I want to do the best I can. When Moyses invited me to sing at his club, I accepted. I learned all the songs that people wanted to hear and I learned how important it was to have a good band. That was how I established myself in cabaret." Elisabeth settled into this exciting new phase in her career with remarkable ease, though at first she experienced some nervousness:

When I began working in cabaret I didn't have stage fright, I had nervousness. My hand would shake when I put my lipstick on but I got over it. It took me a while but I got used to it. I'd had wonderful training in the church choir, and the people I worked with in cabaret in Paris were so friendly and close. I always said "hi" to the boys in the orchestra and the people backstage. I'd stand and shiver in the wings, waiting to go on, but once I went on I concentrated on my audience and lost my nerves. When I started in cabaret I sang at tables, espe-cially in Chez Florence, where I knew everybody.

In 1930 Le Boeuf was still one of the most fashionable clubs in Paris, at-tracting intellectuals, and Elisabeth met them all: "The American author

Gertrude Stein and the French artist Jean Cocteau were among those I met. They were the Paris equivalent of London's Bloomsbury Set." Now and again Moyses released Elisabeth to sing in Chez Florence, one of the smartest night clubs in Paris:

All the film and Broadway stars used to go to Chez Florence. I remember Hollywood film stars like Betty Compson, Gloria Swanson, and Charlie Chaplin coming there. One night Paul Robeson came in and sat at the bar and that was the first time I said hello to him. We had the mayor of New York, Jimmy Walker, who was very famous in those days. All of café society from London and elsewhere came, and I sang. It was marvellous. At Chez Florence I was very young and very excited about singing nightly to a room full of titled Europeans, Britain's lords and ladies, American heiresses and society hostesses, and great names in both theatre and films. I watched them all, watched their elegance, their poise, how they walked in their beautiful gowns, how they talked, drank, and smoked. I even taught myself how to smoke with a packet of cheap cigarettes and a large jug of black coffee to steady me when I felt dizzy. I never used stage make-up. I only used street make-up. I'd put a little more rouge on my cheeks, perhaps. When I bought my first pair of eye lashes I thought I was Josephine Baker because they were long. I did some extra blinking to let the audience see those! I began to take stock of myself. I wanted to be at ease and as elegant as the beautiful women who came into Chez Florence, to move with grace and assurance as well as sing. I started spending on my clothes and it was in Paris that I learned how to wear the latest fashions. With each new gown I felt a new glow. I was complimented on my appearance as well as my singing. I was very happy! In those days everybody was aching to have couture dresses copied. There was a little woman on the outskirts of Paris and she had contacts with girls at one or two of the great fashion houses. They would sneak one of the paper patterns out to her for a night, and she would trace it. Then she would put, for instance, a Patou top and a Lelong skirt together, and that way it wasn't *entirely* a steal. I had a Patou top, I remember, in orange silk, and it had a sort of diamond-shape cut-out in the middle.

One night I was singing in Chez Florence and Jean Patou came in. After the show he invited me over and said, "Look, I don't care if you wear copies of my designs, even if they are with someone else's skirt, but try and find out when I'm coming in and don't wear them for me to see!" Later I would go to him each spring and autumn, and he let me choose one dress from each collection. He told me I should wear only navy blue or white. I don't care for navy blue so I always wore white. That often happened in the good days of Paris. *Artistes* were given everything, from a car to a mink coat by firms who were happy to see their products used or worn by stars. I got no cars or minks but I did get gowns from Patou! It was I who wore them with joy and pride. I never let them wear me. I showed them off. I didn't allow them to show me off! That is the secret of the elegant and poised woman.

Mabel Mercer was, perhaps, the greatest cabaret star of her generation, and Elisabeth followed her into Chez Florence. Mercer had moved to another popular club, Bricktop's. English-born of mixed-race parentage in London's West End, she had appeared in *Blackbirds* (1926) with Florence Mills and *Show Boat* (1928) with Paul Robeson. Mercer later settled in New York, where she influenced some of the great singers of the twentieth century. Frank Sinatra, Billie Holiday, Judy Garland, and Barbara Cook were among them. Elisabeth and Mercer became pals: "Mabel was a great, great friend of mine. She was one of the first people I met when I went to Paris. She was born in England and we used to laugh because she became a big thing in New York and I became popular in England."

Bricktop, who had been born Ada Beatrice Queen Victoria Louise Virginia Smith, was one of the most celebrated nightclub owners in the world. Though she was African American, her racial origins were a curiosity to those who met her, including Elisabeth:

> You couldn't tell whether Bricktop was white, black or green. She was yellow with brown freckles and red hair. All the greats went to Bricktop's and she was a wonderful hostess. When I visited Bricktop's she would invite me to do a "turn." It was expected if you went to her club and were known to be a cabaret *artiste*. Let's face it, we liked being asked. That's how I got to meet the greats like Chevalier, who was a lot of fun, and Mistinguett, who didn't like me very much. I met Ernest Hemingway and went to one of his cocktail parties with all the great names. I got to know F. Scott Fitzgerald quite well. I didn't meet Picasso because he wasn't a party man—well, not in our set! I did meet the American poet Langston Hughes, at Bricktop's, but I didn't get to know him.

In 1930 Elisabeth was offered an engagement to star in cabaret at The Royal Box, a nightclub in New York. She welcomed the opportunity to return home and eagerly accepted. However, during the engagement she came face to face with one of America's top-ten public enemies: "I was singing my songs and in the middle of my act someone said, 'Hold everything.' The musicians stopped and I stopped. That was to allow a party of gangsters to come in while they put the guests out through another door. The gangsters were charming even though they were killers!" A guard stood nearby wearing a fedora and an overcoat, with his hand inside his pocket. The party's leader was none other than the notorious and elusive Dutch Schultz, and the whole FBI was looking for him:

> The men in the party wore gray suits, badly cut. The ladies were in suits and blouses. They looked like office workers. I'm a snob. At least when it comes to

cabarets! At first I didn't know Dutch Schultz was out there. Before I went on he sent word back to my dressing room to inform me that I only had to sing show songs, spirituals, and Irish songs. He ended the session asking for Schwartz and Dietz's "Give Me Something to Remember You By." Afterwards he handed me a wad of notes and said "split this up with the boys." It turned out to be $200. Everyone had to remain in the club until the group left. It was only then that I learned the identity of the generous tipper. At that point my legs turned into cooked spaghetti.

In 1932 Elisabeth accepted a cabaret engagement in Berlin and met her younger brother John, then studying music in the city. A few years later, following the rise of Hitler and the Nazis, it became impossible for a black entertainer to appear on stage in Germany. When Adelaide Hall accepted an engagement to appear in Berlin in the summer of 1936, she was shocked to find herself shunned and pushed about on the sidewalks. But Elisabeth was a hit. A review by "Arno" in the *Berliner Tribune* (June 28, 1932) raved about her:

> Director Skutetzky proves over and over again in his Biguine establishment in the Luther Strasse that he is a show-man of many grades. . . . Now one sees— for the first time in Berlin of course—a wonderful black singer in the Biguine: Elisabeth Welch (please, dear public, don't forget this name, it will yet often be under discussion!). This Madame Welch is harmony "in corpore," a delicate dreamlike experience [*Erlebnis*] when she opens her mouth, when her marvellous teeth glisten and she captivates even the greatest snob among her audience with her songs which go to the heart. "Love for Sale" she sings—and one feels that her representation of the love-slave who has to sell her love, becomes startling reality through Elisabeth Welch. Many new American "*chansons*" are sliding over the lips of this highly gifted black woman, and when she sings in German parody-language, there comes a warming shine from our mother-tongue as if it had obtained romantic charm. I find this Elisabeth Welch, a creole of the noblest kind, so bewitching that I cannot help signifying her as one of the few attractions of our present Varieté-Berlin.

When Elisabeth sailed between New York and Paris between 1929 and 1932, she always travelled on what she described as the "big ships": "I paid my fare but as soon as they saw on my passport 'artist' or if they knew I was an artist, they'd offer me a nice suite in First Class. So I always travelled First Class with a Third Class fare, but, of course, I had to give a ship's concert in return—which was easy!"

~

CHAPTER FOUR

Cole Porter, Ivor Novello, and Noël Coward

A Classy Lady

During her cabaret engagement at The Royal Box, Elisabeth was given a copy of Cole Porter's "Love for Sale," a prostitute's lament, by her friend Peggy Hopkins Joyce, a major American celebrity of the era. Peggy advised her to include the song in her act. Elisabeth described Hopkins Joyce as "a former Ziegfeld girl and a very elegant, charming woman. She was a glamorous person who was kept by millionaires. She brought me this sheet of music and said, 'Elisabeth, you should learn this song by Cole Porter because it's from one of his shows, and it's coming into Broadway.'" In those days singers were permitted to include show songs in their act prior to the opening of the show: "So I learned it, and put it in my repertoire and then the show opened." For many years the lyrics of "Love for Sale" could not be broadcast on American radio. Perhaps because it was so badly treated, Porter referred to it as his favourite among all the songs he wrote: "I like it best because it's kind of a step-child. . . . I can't understand it. You can write a novel about a harlot, paint a picture of a harlot, but you can't write a song about a harlot." For Elisabeth, "it was beautiful poetry because it was like one of the street cries of London."

Elisabeth was the first to sing "Love for Sale," before it was officially launched by Kathryn Crawford in *The New Yorkers* when it opened at the

Broadway Theatre on December 8, 1930, but there was such an outcry that it was decided Crawford had to be replaced:

> It was ridiculous. "Love for Sale" was the song of a prostitute and they gave it to a little pink and white blonde girl. She looked like a pretty schoolgirl, which was entirely wrong for this kind of song. She was totally unsuitable for such a number and the critics slated it. One described it as filthy. You'd think with Monty Woolley directing, E. Ray Goetz producing, and Cole Porter writing the songs, they wouldn't have allowed it. When I went to see the show, I was shocked. The critics attacked "Love for Sale" so much that Cole Porter left for Paris in a rage three days after the show opened. So they realised they had to replace her.

One night, about two or three in the morning, Elisabeth was leaving The Royal Box to go home when someone asked her to take her coat off because three gentlemen had arrived and asked to hear her sing "Love for Sale." So Elisabeth went out and sang it for the three men, who turned out to be Monty Woolley, E. Ray Goetz, and a friend, the famous composer and lyricist Irving Berlin. They had come to "audition" Elisabeth: "They heard me sing the song in an empty nightclub and then there was a little tête-à-tête. Two or three days later my manager called me up and said they wanted me to go into *The New Yorkers*."

The men were enthusiastic about Elisabeth, but before casting her, Goetz expressed some concern about putting a black singer in the show. "That's no obstacle," said Berlin. "She's a wonderful singer and if you want her in the show you can always find the right spot for her." That's what they did, after recommending her to Cole Porter, who was in Paris. Porter, without seeing or hearing her, gave his consent.

The setting for "Love for Sale" was originally Madison Avenue, but when Elisabeth joined the cast in January 1931 this had to be altered:

> So they changed Madison Avenue to Lenox Avenue in Harlem, and Reuben's Restaurant to the Cotton Club, and I walked on. I wasn't tough then but I said I wasn't going to go out looking like some floozy. I wanted to portray her as a classy lady—not a tramp—and I knew how I wanted to dress. I'd just come from Paris, what the heck! So I got myself a black satin dress, patent leather black shoes with three-inch red heels, a great big full marabou stole, a big red handbag and a little red hat on the top of my head with black egrets coming out, and I felt mighty good!

In 1931 racism prevented black women appearing on the American stage unless they played maids or streetwalkers, but Elisabeth didn't mind appearing as a prostitute on this occasion. She saw *The New Yorkers* as an opportunity to sing a great Cole Porter song. Her African American contemporaries Florence Mills (*Greenwich Village Follies*, 1923) and Ethel Waters (*As Thousands Cheer*, 1933) (see chapter 2) are often cited as the first to integrate with white casts on Broadway. However, Elisabeth's appearance in *The New Yorkers* is overlooked because she lacked the fame in America of Mills and Waters and because she was a replacement, not in the original cast.

An offer to play a featured role in one of Porter's shows in London's West End meant that *The New Yorkers* would be Elisabeth's last appearance in New York until 1980, and her last on the Broadway stage until 1986. The West End offer came when Elisabeth met Porter after *The New Yorkers* had closed and she had returned to Paris:

> I say to people Cole Porter talked to *me* and they don't believe me because in those days I wouldn't approach *anybody*. I wasn't pompous. I just didn't know how to approach people, especially people like Cole Porter. He came to see me at Chez Florence and afterwards called me up at the club. When someone told me that Cole Porter was on the phone, wanting to speak to me, I said "You're joking!" He asked me to come to his apartment to hear me sing. I accepted the invitation, knowing I was going to meet a great man. He was a meek, quiet little man with wonderful, doe-like eyes. If he had been much smaller you could have hugged him like a little dog or cat. In company he was very shy and withdrawn, not at all gregarious. His wit really came out in his songs. There was no aggression about him, only gentleness, but you could feel strength behind it. He was absolutely charming. He asked me to sing "Love for Sale" with him playing, which was terrible, because he wasn't what you'd call an accompanist. A year later he sent for me again. He was writing a show for Gertrude Lawrence and he had a song for me.

Early in 1933 Elisabeth was singing in Paris when Porter invited her to audition for his new show *Nymph Errant* at his seventeenth-century house at 13 Rue Monsieur. When Elisabeth arrived, Porter's wife Linda, who was about to leave, rudely ignored her: "Linda Porter didn't like me and I didn't like her. She was beautiful but pompous." Afterwards Elisabeth learned that Linda had grown up in the American South: "She probably thought I should be in the cotton fields, not a chic Paris nightclub, and certainly not in one of her husband's shows!"

Porter told Elisabeth he had "dreamed up" a song called "Solomon" after travelling in Turkey, where a sultan had invited him for coffee. Away in the distance Porter had heard the wail of the concubines in the sultan's harem and immediately wrote down the melody, which became "Solomon." At the audition he sang it for Elisabeth: "He had a terrible voice, slightly high-pitched."

Porter had been asked to write the score for *Nymph Errant* by Charles B. Cochran, the famous theatre producer, who was described as Britain's Florenz Ziegfeld. On October 1, 1933, a rehearsal of *Nymph Errant*, introduced by Cochran, was broadcast to America from His Majesty's Theatre, and the show opened at the Adelphi Theatre on October 6. Elisabeth met Gertrude Lawrence, the star of the show, at a cocktail party organised by Cochran for the cast to introduce themselves to each other. She described "Gertie" as "adorable" and "a great star":

> Gertie was glamour and elegance personified. She was such a civilised, human person. I looked at her in awe, until we got to know each other. She had her moods—and who hasn't? She was a person of many faces and moods. One moment she was the star, aloof and in quite a different world, and the next moment she'd be the comedienne telling us jokes and stories in the broadest cockney. She could be withdrawn and worried one day, and full of humour and laughter the next. I liked her very much, and enjoyed the little scene in the harem I had with her before I sang "Solomon," the song that has become my unofficial signature tune. When she was joyful she'd come round to my dressing room and say "Allo, 'ow are you?" in her cockney accent and she always answered her own phone. Now, this was a woman who had maids but she was so curious she'd rush to the 'phone and say "Allo" in her cockney maid voice. When I asked her why she did this she replied, "In case I didn't want to talk to them. I'd say, 'She's not in. Call back later.'" When I went to New York right after the war and she was playing in *Pygmalion* on Broadway, a mutual friend told her that I was in town. The play was sold out, but Gertie sent me two tickets. So I called her to thank her, and she answered the 'phone with "Allo" and I replied "Oh, for God's sake Gertie, you're not still at that again?" She fell about laughing.

In *Nymph Errant* Lawrence played Evangeline Edwards, a girl fresh from finishing school who decides to experiment with life before settling down. Said Elisabeth: "It was based on James Laver's book in which the heroine goes round the world. Actually in the book she has sex all over the world, but in the show she always got away at the last minute!" In those days, everybody pulled together to make the show work:

> In Manchester, where we rehearsed and opened at the Opera House [on September 11], we worked until three or four in the morning, slogging away but there was a camaraderie—that was the joy of working in musicals then. Cole Porter and Charles B. Cochran came to every rehearsal. They'd take off their coats and sit in their shirt-sleeves with everybody else, and send out for coffee

and sandwiches. That was before the days of Equity rules and we would re-hearse until the early hours of the morning! It was lovely, very *en famille*. Cole was always the gentleman. He didn't stand up and hug you. It wasn't forced, just warm and natural. Stage hands always have a good instinct for the real people, and all the stage hands adored him because he treated everybody as a lady or a gentleman. They loved Charles B. Cochran too. I was featured as Haidee Robinson, a traveller. In the centre of the stage was this enormous satin poof and Gertie, who was so beautiful, had the longest legs. She didn't sit, she languished! The eunuch brings me on and Gertie said "Where did you come from?" and I replied "I was travelling and I lost my ticket. Somebody found me and brought me to this harem." That's how I made my entrance in *Nymph Errant*. Then I launched into "Solomon." Gertie continued languishing on a big pile of pillows while the girls in the back in golden cages ate fruit and looked at themselves in mirrors.

Elisabeth's rendition of "Solomon" stopped the show and endeared her to British theatre-goers. Her scrapbook includes letters of appreciation from Cochran and Porter. She said: "After the opening night show, when I walked into the Savoy Grill for supper, I was knocked off my feet when everyone in the room applauded my entrance." *Nymph Errant* was a success, though at the time critics preferred Porter's *Gay Divorce*, with Fred Astaire, which was then playing in London, at the Palace.

Nymph Errant closed on February 17, 1934, after a brief run of only 154 performances in just over four months, but Elisabeth always kept Porter's "Love for Sale," "Solomon," and "Experiment" (performed by Gertrude Lawrence in *Nymph Errant*) in her repertoire. When asked about Porter, she always acknowledged the wit and elegance of his songs, which suited her, es-pecially in cabaret and, later, her one-woman concerts: "Irving Berlin wrote for the general public but Cole for a much more sophisticated audience."

After beginning his career as a composer, Ivor Novello won international fame as a star of the silent screen. From 1935 until his death in 1951, he cre-ated a series of highly popular British operettas. These were noted for their lush music, bittersweet stories, and romantic settings. Christopher Hassall was the lyricist for six of them, and Novello, who did not sing, acted in six, including the first, *Glamorous Night*. After seeing Elisabeth in *Nymph Errant* he decided to cast her in *Glamorous Night* as a stowaway called Cleo Welling-ton. The show opened at the Theatre Royal, Drury Lane, on May 2, 1935. Elisabeth later expressed her admiration for the composer:

Ivor Novello was a great romantic and always going to the opera. He took me to my first opera. I heard Grace Moore of all people doing Mimi, and she was dreadful. I don't think Ivor would be accepted particularly now, because of what some people would call his schmaltz but I don't say schmaltz. I call it romance. Ivor was a man who was in love with love. I'm a singer that goes around the house singing all the time and I never know what I've been singing until I've stopped, and I always find myself singing Ivor's "Shine through My Dreams." It's so romantic, and it's stayed with me all through the years. So his music has lasted, for me anyway. I hadn't met him before *Glamorous Night*, but he knew my work. He called me up one day and he said "If I write a song for you will you come and join *Glamorous Night?*" I said "What's *Glamorous Night?*" He said "A musical starring Mary Ellis and myself. Oliver Messel will be designing the sets." I said "Of course I'll do it" without even hearing the songs he wrote for me, and I was already a fan of Mary Ellis. After arriving in London I went to see her in Jerome Kern's *Music in the Air* at His Majesty's. She overwhelmed me with her glorious singing and I was overwhelmed again when I realised I was to be in *Glamorous Night* with her. I had one number in each of the two acts. "Far Away in Shanty Town" in the first and "The Girl I Knew" in the second. They're not in the script. They're not in the score, either. Ivor just put me there as a stowaway dressed in rags on board a ship who is dragged on to sing "Shanty Town" at the ship's concert. Later, during a difficult scene change in Act 2, I went on in front of the curtain, this time dressed in a chic Victor Stiebel costume, and sang "The Girl I Knew."

On the opening night everyone came dressed up, and Elisabeth peeked through the curtains to see who was coming in, especially anyone of importance. Hearing extra-loud applause she looked out to see Marlene Dietrich on the arm of Douglas Fairbanks, Jr:

> Marlene looked seven million dollars. She'd been filming and she came to the theatre in dark make-up and she had a white dress on, and she was blonde. And there she was with Dougie Fairbanks Jr., a beautiful prince, walking down the aisle with the audience applauding. Well, Ivor's mother, Clara Novello Davies, was up in the Royal Box, and she had been attracting all the attention up to then. Suddenly there was a big rush of papers and a large box of chocolates had been tipped over the side and into the audience, so of course they were distracted and all looked up at Ivor's mother. Marlene and Dougie had to get to their seats very quickly!

Elisabeth enjoyed working with Ivor Novello and taking part in *Glamorous Night*, but one matter concerned her. A lack of confidence prevented her from speaking out. Christopher Hassall had included the word "nigger" in his lyric to "Far Away in Shanty Town," and this upset Elisabeth: "At every performance, when I started to sing 'Shanty Town,' though I loved the song, I went cold as that line came closer. I hated it, but I said nothing about it to anyone. I was new to Britain and I loved everyone connected with the show, especially Ivor. I didn't want to upset him, or rock any boats. Perhaps I should have done but after the show ended its run I did change the lyric whenever I sang the song again."

Ivor Novello and Noël Coward effectively ran English musical theatre between the wars. Almost every major hit came from one or other of them. Mary Ellis once described them as "friendly enemies." Said Elisabeth:

> In 1946, when Noël was putting on *Pacific 1860* at Drury Lane, Ivor said to me "Are you going to the dress rehearsal?" I said, "Yes. I have a front row seat." He said, "You're coming with me to the Ivy restaurant afterwards and you've got to tell me everything that happens because I've told Noël there are a lot of things he shouldn't do in it and he won't listen. I want to hear what's going to happen." But he said all of this with a sort of joy, a bitch joy which we all have occasionally.

Elisabeth once explained that she remained friends with Noël Coward because she never worked for him:

> He was a terrible perfectionist. He wanted people to do things exactly the way he did them. Well, no artist who's an artist can do an imitation. I couldn't imitate his sort of word sections or the inflections not only of the music but of the lyric. I have to read my story and sing it my way. I'm not talking only about me. All artists, if they've got any sense, do that, but Noël and I always got along marvellously, but then, you see, I never worked for him. He once said to me at a party, "Lis, it's amazing we've known each other all these years, and yet we've never worked together," and I told him, "That's probably why we get along so well!" I'd seldom seen Noël taken aback before, but not with dislike. He was surprised, because everybody worshiped him. I worshiped him, too. I'd known him since Paris, when he was a pompous so-and-so. I have no fear of anybody, especially if I can answer back.

Elisabeth and Coward did take part together in *Jubilee Gala*, an all-star radio programme for the BBC on July 27, 1935. The line-up also included Gertrude Lawrence and the American comedienne Charlotte Greenwood. For an all-star celebration for Coward's seventieth birthday at the Phoenix Theatre on December 16, 1969, Elisabeth performed his song "Twentieth Century Blues" (from Coward's 1931 stage success *Cavalcade*). Elisabeth so impressed The Master with her interpretation that afterwards he remarked that it was the first time he had ever heard it performed as he had originally visualised it. This was praise indeed from such a "terrible perfectionist"!

In her living-room at Capener's Close, Elisabeth proudly displayed a bust of Coward by Gladys Calthrop. On December 8, 1987, the journalist Patrick

Newley and the photographer Colin Bourner had visited her. During Newley's interview with the star, Bourner suddenly caught sight of the bust of
Coward. "What are you looking at?" asked Elisabeth. "Oh, Miss Welch, I was
just admiring your bust," replied Bourner. "Well, honey, you must have good
eyesight because my bust isn't what it used to be!" she said, roaring with
laughter. "Oh, you're looking at Noël," she added. "You know he was a real
pain in the ass. Still, we were friends and that's what counts, isn't it?"

Throughout her career Elisabeth was associated with a number of famous
gay men in the arts, especially in the worlds of film and musical theatre.
Apart from Porter, Novello, and Coward, she was directed on film by Brian
Desmond Hurst (see chapter 7) and Derek Jarman (see chapter 9). She was
also directed by Alberto Cavalcanti, in the Ealing classic *Dead of Night*
(1945) (see chapter 7). During the war she entertained the troops with John
Gielgud (see chapter 7) and the female impersonator Douglas Byng, whom
she described as "my first camp friend and a lovely cabaret artist." After the
war, Laurier Lister devised and directed three of her most successful revues
(see chapter 8). Peter Wildeblood, the journalist, novelist, and gay-rights
campaigner, wrote the book and lyrics for one of her greatest personal successes, *The Crooked Mile* (1959) (see chapter 8).

Of Cole Porter she said, "Everyone in the theatre knew he was homosex-
ual, but it was not discussed." This was Elisabeth's view on the subject. She
rarely commented on the sexuality of the gay men she worked with. It was a
matter of respecting the privacy of her friends and associates, and of being
discreet, especially in Britain, where male homosexuality was against the law
until partially decriminalised in 1967. The private lives of the gay men she
befriended—or worked with—remained as private as her own off-stage life.

CHAPTER FIVE

~

Soft Lights and Sweet Music

One Song Welch

Elisabeth arrived in London in May 1933, but *Nymph Errant* (see chapter 4) was not due to go into rehearsals until August. In Paris she had featured Harold Arlen and Ted Koehler's torch song "Stormy Weather" in her cabaret act. Ethel Waters had just introduced "Stormy Weather" at the Cotton Club, and ten years later Lena Horne would popularise the song when she sang it in a Hollywood film, also called *Stormy Weather*. On her arrival in London, Elisabeth was offered a part in a revue called *Dark Doings*, which opened on June 26 at the Leicester Square Theatre. The cast included some performers from the Cotton Club in New York whom Elisabeth had met in Paris. They included Alma Smith, Areta Day, the Five Hot Shots, Roy Atkins, Brookins and Van, Jazz Lips Richardson, and Henry Wessels: "They were lovely dancing girls and comics but when they came to London to open a revue, they needed a 'name' so they asked me to join them as their lead singer." Elisabeth saw *Dark Doings* as an opportunity to introduce "Stormy Weather" to Britain. However, before she could sign the contract she had to seek permission from Charles B. Cochran, who had already contracted her for *Nymph Errant*:

He called me to his office in New Bond Street and within minutes he asked if I knew Nina Mae McKinney, another coloured artist who'd been successful in his famous revues at the Trocadero. He spoke with amusement of some of her flare-ups. She thought that to be a star you must be temperamental and nasty. Cochran said he gave her money to bury her father at least four times and her mother twice. I realised he was wondering what I'd be like. He thought he was getting another demon like Nina. However, he soon realised I was nothing like her, and changed the subject. He then talked about the late Florence Mills who took London by storm in *Dover Street to Dixie*, his show of the early 1920s. He adored her. In fact, I was happy when, the following November, he chose me to sing her hit song "Silver Rose" on a recording of some of his show hits. Then he said "tell me about this show that you want to go into." When I told him it was a revue at the Leicester Square Theatre he said "that's not a theatre. That's a music hall. It has nothing to do with the West End or my productions!" So he gave me permission to appear in *Dark Doings*. The interview over, we shook hands and I knew I was going to like working for him. So I introduced "Stormy Weather" to Britain. I beat Duke Ellington by two weeks because he came over with that fantastic band of his and that lovely singer Ivie Anderson and one of their big features was "Stormy Weather."

The first half of *Dark Doings* was performed by a white cast, the second half by a black cast. One of the highlights of the show was Elisabeth singing "Stormy Weather" in a shanty-town set, complete with thunder rolling and lightning flashing: "I don't know how I got through the song because the production was so funny. Unfortunately it was the summer of 1933, one of the hottest summers I've ever lived through, and people didn't want to be indoors, so this success only lasted about three weeks. It was gruelling." Elisabeth found *Dark Doings* tough going, for in addition to the hot weather she had to perform in four shows a day: "I hadn't done it before and I haven't done it since," she later said.

The majority of black performers who appeared in Broadway shows and nightclubs during the Harlem Renaissance of the 1920s found popularity and acclaim in Britain. They were featured in recordings, music halls, cabaret, West End revues, radio, and, almost without exception, British films or television. The blues singer Alberta Hunter, who had played opposite Paul Robeson in *Show Boat* at the Theatre Royal, Drury Lane in 1928, explained: "We went to Europe because we were recognized and given a chance. In Europe they had your name up in lights. People in the United States would not give us that chance." It is hardly surprising, then, that historian Jeffrey Green suggests in his essay "The Negro Renaissance in England" (see bibliography) that in Britain another "Harlem Renaissance" took place, in particular after the economic crash of 1929: "The occurrence of a Harlem Renaissance in England seems unlikely, if not absurd, but New York did not have the sole possession of the ideas that led to the black artistic outflow of the Renaissance."

It is important to acknowledge that some black entertainers who worked in Britain between the two world wars received not only acclaim and popularity but also positions in high society. In fact, the association of black entertainers with Britain's upper classes and royalty can be traced back to the Victorian era, when African Americans gave command performances for the queen. These included the Fisk Jubilee Singers, a choral group famous for performing Negro spirituals, and the renowned concert singer Elizabeth Taylor Greenfield. The African American cast of *In Dahomey*, led by Bert Williams and George Walker and staged at the Shaftesbury Theatre, was invited to perform for King Edward VII at Buckingham Palace in 1903. However, although such contacts suggest a level of social acceptance, Jeffrey Green reveals that further investigation shows that to be a superficial view,

> for black entertainers were seldom truly accepted as individuals, but in general only as symbols. This led to a paradox, since the association of black people with the aristocratic and ruling elite of Britain was seen in America as a social triumph, and was reported as such in the press, biographies, and autobiographies. . . . If the Americans saw the association of black entertainers and Britain's high society as a black success, it would seem likely that a number of Britons, black and white, would conclude the same. British liberals, aghast at lynching, Jim Crow, and other manifestations of racism in America, could show that the mingling of black people in British high society proved how different life was in Britain. The reality was that black access to high society was as volatile as show business, and friends were as fickle as audiences.

On her arrival here in 1933, Elisabeth discovered she was a member of an exclusive group of African Americans then working and enjoying success in the performing arts in Britain. For instance, in the year Elisabeth made her London debut, Paul Robeson (see chapter 6) appeared at the Embassy Theatre with Flora Robson in an acclaimed production of Eugene O'Neill's drama *All God's Chillun' Got Wings*; the comedy duo Scott and Whaley, who had been music hall stars in Britain for over two decades, was starring in the long-running and popular BBC (British Broadcasting Corporation) radio series *Kentucky Minstrels*; Layton and Johnstone were continuing their reign as a first-class cabaret act; and Nina Mae McKinney topped the bill at the London Palladium. In West End musical theatre, Buddy Bradley had reached a position as one of Britain's foremost choreographers. In 1930 he staged the dances for Charles B. Cochran's hit *Ever Green*, starring Jessie Matthews. In 1934, again choreographing Matthews, he began a short reign in films that earned him the title "Britain's Busby Berkeley." But success didn't come only to African Americans. Born on the island of Grenada in 1900, in what was then known as the British West Indies, in the 1920s and 1930s Leslie "Hutch" Hutchinson proved to be a class act in high society, the top cabaret entertainer of his generation, and the supreme interpreter of Cole Porter's songs. Elisabeth recalled:

> I think I met Hutch in Paris. I knew of him and had seen one or two perform-ances in a nightclub in the Pigalle. He was very well known even before he came to London. Everyone loved Hutch. He was very elegant and flirted with the ladies. He dressed beautifully in Savile Row suits and carried himself as an Englishman. One of his trademarks was the white handkerchief in his left sleeve. Occasionally he pulled it out and patted his face while playing or singing something. He was a lovely person who put on airs, being the grand Englishman, but we didn't mind because he was having fun as well. He had a sense of humour and you can get away with anything in our business if you have a sense of humour. He didn't believe it. He was pulling the leg of the pub-lic and his friends knew this. He had a brother who was the complete opposite and laughed at him as well. I got to know Hutch when we met socially in the marvellous late-night dives of Soho which, in those days, attracted all the stars and theatregoers. We wouldn't think of going home after a performance. That world was very exciting. People really lived. I was scared of Hutch at first but that soon passed. He was very amorous and I wasn't. Anyway, he wasn't my type. He was very nice to me, and we ended up good friends. That was impor-tant to me. We used to have a lot of giggles, because he would tell me a lot of stories about himself and his flirtations. He gave the impression that he always woke up with a smile. He was never miserable.

Reginald Foresythe was London-born of Nigerian-German ancestry and had a reputation as a jazz innovator as great as Duke Ellington's. Following her appearances in *Dark Doings* and *Nymph Errant*, Elisabeth began accept-ing cabaret and variety engagements, but she needed an accompanist. To her great surprise, someone suggested Reginald Foresythe. She was more sur-prised when he accepted:

> Reggie is a favourite of mine because when I came to London and I had cabaret and variety engagements I didn't know anyone as an accompanist. I was given his name and I thought "it can't be *the* Reggie Foresythe." I'd heard about him in America and Paris with his "Serenade for a Wealthy Widow." I heard about him in New York when he came over to play with Paul Whiteman, who was known as the King of Jazz. I didn't think Reggie would want to play for me. He was the most sweet, simple, charming person. Elegant and loved good food and always talked in a grand way, but he had a great sense of humour about him-self. We used to send him up. He didn't mind it at all. We all laughed. I used to go about two or three times a week to the famous 400 Club where he ap-peared with his band, his "New Music." People always asked for his "Serenade

for a Wealthy Widow." Reggie was ahead of his time, experimenting with popular music and jazz music.

Elisabeth disapproved of being labelled a jazz singer, preferring to be described as a singer of popular songs. However, just a few years after settling in London, she enjoyed a professional encounter in London with Benny Carter, one of the great African American jazz musicians. Elisabeth had grown up in the same Manhattan street as the Carter family and had attended the same school as Benny's sister. On recognising Elisabeth from a photograph he happened to see in a music publisher's office in London, Benny sought out his old childhood friend and persuaded her to make some records with him. In June 1936 Elisabeth joined Carter and his orchestra (credited on some tracks as his Swing Quartet) to record such popular tunes as "When Lights Are Low" and George and Ira Gershwin's "The Man I Love." One of the musicians on the first session—"I Gotta Go"—was the Jamaican trumpeter Leslie Thompson. He was one of the pioneers of jazz in Britain, and he had already played—and recorded—with Louis Armstrong's Paris Band. In *Leslie Thompson: An Autobiography* (1985) he said: "I don't regard Duke Ellington as the grand daddy as I think that Carter has to be the number one. He was the most outstanding coloured musician. He had a wide experience, was polished, could play so many instruments so well, and was above all a fantastic arranger. . . . Carter always had good men but he never had the luck. . . . Carter just kept on trying; he just never got the publicity that Duke and the others got."

In 1934 Elisabeth's agent persuaded her to tour in variety, Britain's equivalent of America's vaudeville. It was one of the most popular forms of entertainment. Following appearances at the London Palladium, with Cab Calloway, and the Holborn Empire, Elisabeth accepted an engagement outside London:

It was a disaster. My agent booked me into Birmingham Hippodrome, of all places. Someone warned me that if they didn't like you, Birmingham audiences sat on their hands to stop themselves from applauding! That was rather frightening. Anyhow I went up there and I opened but, stupidly, because nobody advised me, I was billed as a "West End Star." Well, variety audiences don't want to know about West End stars. Musical-comedy people don't mean a damn thing to them. Even the *artistes* on the bill resented it. I suppose they thought I was going to be posh. Well, I went on and I sang my cabaret numbers which was completely wrong. It was death. I came on and sang my first song, Duke Ellington's "I Let a Song Go Out of My Heart," but there was no applause. So I gave them a big dramatic number, "Don't Let the River Run Dry," all about cotton picking.

Birmingham didn't want to know. When I went off stage after the fourth number, then I got applause. I think they were glad to see me go but I had to come
back for my fifth—and final—song, and I could almost hear them say "Oh, my
God, here she comes again." They were really fed up. I think they were glad to
see me go, but when they saw me coming back I felt this terrible down, and I had
to sing this number. After that I think they waited to see if I was coming back
again and when I didn't I got a big round of applause. Anyhow it taught me an
important lesson because I'd done cabaret and theatre and here I was doing variety which had a completely different feel. You walk onto the stage and if you
don't get your audience immediately—and hold them—you've had it. If they're
not excited and interested, good evening and good night!

In spite of her negative experience in Birmingham, Elisabeth continued
accepting variety engagements, billed as the "Syncopated Songstress" or
"Mistress of Song." She reached a wide audience and shared bills with some
of the great names of British music hall. These included the comedian
George Formby and eccentric dancers Wilson, Keppel, and Betty (Empire
Theatre, Edinburgh, 1935) and comedian Norman Evans (New Theatre,
Cardiff, 1939). She appreciated the lessons it taught her but noted that "it
wasn't friendly and I'm a friendly person. I like to make contact. I never went
into digs, because I didn't know anybody, so I stayed in hotels and it was very
lonely." Elisabeth was more at home in the sophisticated world of cabaret in
London's West End. In 1935 she accepted an offer to sing at the famous Café
de Paris, with Reginald Foresythe as her accompanist:

The London cabaret scene was very sophisticated and my first London engagement was at the Café de Paris which was just off Leicester Square. That
was the grand night club of London and all the big names of cabaret played
there. It was very chic and very smart. I followed Douglas Byng, the wonderful
female impersonator. I loved the place, even though it had a very snooty clien-
tele, but I won them over, nobody was going to undo Welch! The people of
London society, including the Royals, were always part of my life. The Queen
Mother was a great friend of mine. Before her Coronation in 1937, in the days
when she was the Duchess of York, she came to see me at the Café de Paris,
and I sang for her at Windsor, even after she became Queen. At Windsor I had
to sing on the lawn, in the open air, and I hated doing that. You get no resonance. Your voice just goes away but I loved going to Windsor because the
Queen Mother had lovely tea parties. I sang at other Palaces too, including the
Butler's [servants] Ball at Buckingham Palace.

On October 14, 1933, Elisabeth made her debut on BBC radio in *C. B.
Cochran Presents*, a programme arranged by Henry Hall, one of the BBC's top

broadcasters. Cochran acted as *compère* in a selection of song hits from his most popular shows, played by Henry Hall and his famous BBC dance band. Cochran was also introduced and interviewed by Hall. During the broadcast Elisabeth performed "Solomon" from *Nymph Errant*. Her appearance marked the beginning of an association with BBC radio that lasted for over sixty years, until her final broadcast in 1994, when she was interviewed about Florence Mills for *Black in the West End*:

> During 1934 and 1935, when I was singing in a radio series for the BBC called *Soft Lights and Sweet Music*, I was on the air more or less every week for quite a while, so my name became well-known from Scotland down to Devon. There was a small group of musicians, four or five in number, and I was the singing voice. The series was devised by Austen Croom-Johnson. We called him "Ginger." As a result I became a name up and down the country without people ever knowing what I looked like. We used to have to worry a lot about what clothes we wore because, in those days, there was no wardrobe department. We wore our best clothes even when we doing radio things at what we called The Big House, which was Broadcasting House in Portland Place. The BBC was called "Auntie" because it had a reputation for being prim and prissy. The ladies, for example, never had plunges in their dresses—the BBC was very strict about that—and the men, or most of the men, had to wear evening jackets and a black tie. Certainly, all the announcers had to dress like that but we all kept our sense of humour.

In 1936 Elisabeth became a pioneer of a new medium called television: "In north London the BBC started transmissions of something new that was to be a revolution in the entertainment business. Radio with pictures. Television was born, and I was in at the birth!" However, though Elisabeth may have been one of the first black women to appear on the BBC's regular television service, in 1933 both Nina Mae McKinney and Josephine Baker took part in John Logie Baird's experimental broadcasts. In the United States it was Ethel Waters who took the honour of becoming the first black *artiste* to appear on American television, when she starred in *The Ethel Waters Show*, an experimental broadcast for the NBC radio network in 1939.

On November 2, 1936, the talented American double-act Buck and Bubbles made history when they were featured in a variety show on the opening day of the BBC's regular high-definition television service at Alexandra Palace in north London. The *Radio Times* described them as "a coloured pair who are versatile comedians who dance, play the piano, sing and cross-chat." Buck and Bubbles were invited to make their historic appearance because they were starring in the West End revue *Transatlantic Rhythm*. In the pre-war years of BBC television (1936–1939), before the outbreak of war interrupted the service, black singers and dancers made an important contribution to entertainment programmes, and most of them were drawn from West End shows or nightclubs. They included Alberta Hunter, Valaida Snow, Adelaide Hall, Art Tatum, The Mills Brothers, and Paul Robeson.

Elisabeth made her first appearances soon after the opening day in "light musical items," also transmitted from Alexandra Palace:

> At Alexandra Palace we had to step over all those cables that were all over the floor, some of them as big as water hoses like the ones you see in the streets and some very narrow. We had to climb over a whole sea of cables just to get to the camera, and when we got to the camera, which never moved, we just stood there in front of it. The cameras were like the old-fashioned still cameras used to take pictures—the cameraman wore a black hood over his head. We didn't need make-up. It was in black and white, of course, and you just stood there and sang your song. Then you waited until somebody said "cut" or "black out," or whatever, and moved away. It was static, nerve-wracking, but amusing. And, when we had a studio with four or five *artistes* doing a programme, it was chaotic. I mean, we were falling over each other and trying to be quiet at the same time but we had fun. It was wonderful! Of course, you must also remember that everything was live. If we made a mistake, we couldn't just re-do it from scratch and the cameras weren't that reliable. During a play or an evening of *artistes* in a concert-type production, we would be singing away or speaking when suddenly we'd hear "Cut! The camera's gone." Then we'd have to set the scene up again and make a new start but we were all young then, and we could laugh about it.

On January 28, 1938, Elisabeth took part in *Making a Gramophone Record,* one of the BBC's first outside broadcasts. The *Radio Times* explained: "Viewers will see Elisabeth Welch, Robert Ashley, BBC chorus, and the New Mayfair Orchestra recording 'Vocal Gems' of George Gershwin's songs at His Master's Voice studios in St. John's Wood." Elisabeth was billed in the *Radio Times* to appear with Ken "Snakehips" Johnson and His West Indian Dance Orchestra on September 3, 1939, but the transmission was cancelled due to the outbreak of war. The BBC ended its television service on September 1 and did not resume until 1946.

In the early, pre-war days of British television, all programmes were transmitted live, broadcast for just a few hours a day to a limited audience that was exclusively white and middle-class. Also, between 1936 and 1949, the BBC could only broadcast in the London area. A television was an expensive commodity, costing the same as a new car, until the coronation of Elizabeth II in 1953 boosted its popularity, soon after which over half the population owned a set. Sadly, before the invention of videotape, no technology existed to record any of these early transmissions, though one of the BBC's demonstration films, *Television Is Here Again* (1946), featured Elisabeth (see chapter 7). The earliest surviving appearances by Elisabeth are *Music for You* (May 16, 1956), in which she sings Ivor Novello's "Far Away in Shanty Town," and the *Sunday-Night Theatre* presentation of *Mrs. Patterson* (June 17, 1956), in which she co-starred with Eartha Kitt. These live transmissions were filmed onto 35 mm stock from a television monitor, a process known as "telerecording" in Britain and "kinescoping" in the United States.

Throughout the 1930s Elisabeth's name became well known to the British public through her regular appearances on BBC radio and television; the BBC also provided the setting for Elisabeth's first film appearance. In the crime thriller *Death at Broadcasting House* (1934) she sang "Lazy Lady," accompanied by Ord Hamilton at the piano and Chappie D'Amato on the guitar. Elisabeth's only comment on the film was: "It was so awful I told everyone they should have left 'Broadcasting House' out of the title and released it as *Death!*"

Apart from her two starring roles opposite Paul Robeson in *Song of Freedom* (1936) and *Big Fella* (1937) (see chapter 6), Elisabeth was given little to do in British films in the 1930s other than sing songs in cabaret or nightclub sequences. She said: "I was in a few films, but I wasn't a star. I only appeared as myself but I enjoyed appearing in them because the other people in the films made it so special for me." After *Death at Broadcasting House* Elisabeth's other "one-song" film appearances included three low-budget musical revues featuring a host of variety acts and bands: *Soft Lights and Sweet Music* (1936), *Calling All Stars* (1937), and the now-lost *Around the Town* (1938). She was also featured in a sparkling early Technicolor comedy, *Over the Moon* (1937).

In the "Harlem Holiday" segment of *Calling All Stars* Elisabeth performed a haunting blues number called "Nightfall," with music by Benny Carter. Set in the Cotton Club (courtesy of a film studio in Beaconsfield, not the real thing in New York!), this wonderful sequence also featured the sophisticated singer-pianist Turner Layton with "These Foolish Things," Buck and Bubbles with "The Rhythm's OK in Harlem," and the Nicholas Brothers (Harold and Fayard) with a Cab Calloway–type number called "Za Zu Za Zu," followed by one of their greatest on-screen tap dance routines. The "Harlem Holiday" segment of *Calling All Stars* showcased some of the best African American talent then working in Britain, and none of the artists were demeaned. For instance, in the film Turner Layton and the Nicholas Brothers are dressed in tuxedos, Elisabeth looks stunning in her shimmering silver gown, and the black musicians in the background look classy.

Over the Moon was co-directed by William K. Howard and Thornton Freeland, who spent several years directing films in Britain. One of Freeland's
previous directorial assignments was *Flying Down to Rio* (1933), featuring
Fred Astaire and Ginger Rogers in their first on-screen partnership. It was in
this musical extravaganza that the lovely African American singer Etta
Moten performed the Oscar-nominated song "Carioca." In Britain Freeland
directed Paul Robeson in the adventure-drama *Jericho* (1937). In *Over the
Moon* Elisabeth made a lively appearance (in a role billed on the cast list as
"cabaret singer") in a fictitious Monte Carlo nightclub, the "Dixie Club." An
unidentified newspaper cutting in her scrapbook describes the filming of this
memorable sequence:

> All the studio seemed to have business on stage one when Elisabeth Welch was
> recording "Red Hot Annabelle" at Denham. This new and specially composed
> rumba was put over by the famous coloured singer with terrific punch. A hun-
> dred of London's smartest extras also listened to her singing of this rumba com-
> posed by Mischa Spoliansky. At a table close to the small dance floor sat Merle
> Oberon with Louis Borell, Ursula Jeans and Zena Dare. The orchestra for her
> song has been assembled by London Films' musical director, Muir Mathieson,
> and consisted of such famous players as Rudy Sarita with the xylophone,
> marimba and vibraphone, Sam Gellesley with his guitar and Jimmy Blades, for-
> mer drummer with Charlie Kunz.

However, Elisabeth was unimpressed by the on-set behaviour of the star
of the film—Merle Oberon—who at that time was the mistress of the film's
producer, Alexander Korda (they married in 1939): "She was temperamental and difficult. I haven't forgotten the time she asked a young, nervous assistant to bring her some gloves. When he returned with the wrong pair, she
blew her top, and had him fired on the spot. I suppose being the mistress of
Alexander Korda she could get away with that sort of behaviour, but she
liked me, thank goodness, and invited me into her tent on the set to sing for
her and Korda, a lovely man." Though she disapproved of Oberon's behaviour on the set, Elisabeth was aware of what she must have been experienc-
ing, being mixed-race and passing for white: "We all knew that the little Indian lady who lived with her in her London apartment was really her
mother, even though Merle told everyone she was her *ayah* [maidservant]
but if the press had found out the truth about Merle, her career would have
been ruined." Oberon's true racial identity was an open secret in some show
business circles, but it was kept from the public until 1983, a few years after
her death, when *Merle*, Charles Higham and Roy Moseley's biography, was
published.

After *Glamorous Night,* Elisabeth made her fourth appearance in a West End show when she joined the cast of *Let's Raise the Curtain.* Opening at the Victoria Palace on September 28, 1936, the show was not a happy experience: "I try to forget about *Let's Raise the Curtain.* It was an absolute mess except for Florence Desmond's brilliant impersonations of Marlene Dietrich, Jessie Matthews, Greta Garbo, and Katharine Hepburn. The producer was Kurt Robitschek, but we used to call him 'Rubber Check' for obvious reasons! It was supposed to be a revue but he stuck a miniature operetta in the whole of the Second Act called 'Beautiful Galatea'! I left out *Let's Raise the Curtain* when they were doing my entry for *Who's Who in the Theatre*—but they put it in anyway." Elisabeth made her fifth West End appearance in *It's in the Bag,* a happier affair than her previous venture. The revue opened at the Saville Theatre on November 4, 1937: "*It's in the Bag* got some marvellous notices, including a good one from James Agate—and praise from Agate was praise indeed—but I do not know what happened. The public just did not come. We held on for about three months and then closed." Alan Bott, reviewing the show in *The Tatler* (November 24, 1937), acknowledged Elisabeth's versatility—"singing expressively in three styles, the huskily passionate, the intensively yearning and the Harlem café-au-lait."

In the 1930s, summer shows were the equal of anything produced in London's West End: "I did my first one at the Opera House in Blackpool from June to October 1938. It was a production called *All the Best* and we had a marvellous cast including Anton Dolin, Stanley Holloway, George Lacey, and Betty Driver. George Black, our producer, bought spectacular sets from the Folies Bergère that year and he built our show around them. The big finale involved fans, feathers, and showgirls. The entire cast, over forty of us, must have been on the stage. It was a big success."

Elisabeth's *All the Best* co-star and understudy, Betty Driver, went on to become a popular vocalist with Henry Hall and his orchestra, and in 1969 she made her first appearance as the cheerful barmaid Betty Turpin in *Coronation Street,* Britain's most popular television soap opera. In 1985 she paid tribute to Elisabeth in British television's *This Is Your Life:* "I was just a slip of a girl of eighteen when I was booked to play your understudy in a wonderful show called *All the Best* at Blackpool Opera House and every night I used to stand in the wings and listen to your lovely voice. Honestly, nobody could match the elegance of you with your beautiful gowns and performance."

CHAPTER SIX

~

Paul Robeson

The gods were shining down.

Apart from attending a couple of his concerts, Elisabeth hadn't seen Paul Robeson since their brief encounter at the Chez Florence in Paris in 1930. Then, on the morning of May 18, 1936, her phone rang. She was livid, because she was a late riser. It was HMV (His Master's Voice), the famous record company, asking if she would come out to its studios in London's Abbey Road to make a record with Robeson:

> The call came through at half past ten, and I didn't know quite where I was. I said "Do you want Elisabeth Welch?" and the voice replied "Yes" and I said "What do you want me to sing?" He replied "Well, Paul Robeson has a recording session this morning and amongst his songs is a duet." While Paul's orchestrations were being checked they found out that one of them was "I Still Suits Me," the song which Oscar Hammerstein II and Jerome Kern had written for the screen version of *Show Boat*. Of course I agreed to join them—after lunch!

The film version of *Show Boat* had just premiered at Radio City Hall in New York City on May 14, 1936, and Robeson had sung "I Still Suits Me" in the film with Hattie McDaniel, but the song hadn't been commercially recorded, and the film hadn't been released in Britain:

> I arrived at two o'clock in the afternoon, and was taken into the studio. Before I could be introduced to Paul he stalked across the floor, threw his arms wide

open, and gave me the biggest hug. I thought to myself, "Well, isn't this wonderful. I'm in the arms of a friendly bear!" By the time I recovered, I had lost
the nerves I had arrived with. Paul received me with such love, this giant saying "Welcome" and squashing me to his bosom. He really didn't know his own
strength, and I loved him from then on. I absolutely adored him. He was full
of warmth, joy, and happiness. The gods were shining down on me because I'd
met the great one. Anyhow, we had a lot of fun recording the song. It was a
crazy situation because here I was being asked to sing a duet with the great man
and I didn't even know the song! I had to record it by reading it off the music
sheet and that's why I'm singing so high because we didn't have time to change
the key. Afterwards he requested me to play his wife in the film *Song of Freedom*. Nina Mae McKinney was originally cast, but there were difficulties because Paul and Nina had just ended the affair they started during the filming
of *Sanders of the River*.

Treated as an outcast in America, the country of his birth, the actor,
singer, and political activist Paul Robeson had settled in Britain in the late
1920s, where he remained—with several working trips to the United
States—until the outbreak of World War II. At the height of his popularity,
in the 1930s, Robeson became one of Britain's most popular film personalities. Between 1935 and 1940 he starred in six British feature films and was
given top billing in all of them. However, if Robeson was one of the most
popular actors of the 1930s, he probably suffered more disappointments than
any other leading actor of his generation. Black characters in American cinema of the period rarely moved beyond Al Jolson in blackface or the dim-
witted buffoons played by black comedy actors like Stepin Fetchit. For the
ambitious Robeson, the going was tough. There were hardly any opportunities to play challenging roles. Even so, in all of his films, whatever their mer-
its, he succeeded in bringing intelligence, strength, and compassion to his
characters.

When Robeson became a major star in Britain, he negotiated for screen
roles that projected a positive image of a black man, roles that broke away
from one-dimensional and offensive racial stereotypes, but he often found
himself in conflict with an industry that glorified the British Empire and
colonialism. This was certainly the case with his first commercial film,
Sanders of the River (1935), one of a cycle of imperial adventures produced by
Alexander Korda for London Films. Robeson was hurt and embarrassed by
the version of the film that Korda released to the public.

Though Robeson publicly disowned *Sanders of the River*, he believed that
the British film industry had something to offer and continued acting in
British films for several years. For his next project, *Song of Freedom* (1936),

directed by J. Elder Wills, the star insisted on a clause in his contract that gave him the right to approve the final editing of the production.

James Elder Wills had been born of Scottish and Irish parents in London in 1900 and educated at Christ's College and London University. After serving in World War I, he became a scenic artist at the Theatre Royal, Drury Lane. Entering the film industry in the silent era, he worked as an art director for several years before graduating to director on *Tiger Bay* (1933), starring the popular Chinese-American film actress Anna May Wong. His subsequent films as director included two starring Elisabeth and Robeson: *Song of Freedom* (1936) and *Big Fella* (1937). Elisabeth remembered very little about Wills: "I'm afraid I didn't have the knowledge to be interested in him, nor was I interested. I just thought he was a known director. He was a charming man and that's all I know. You see, one knew of Cavalcanti [who directed Elisabeth in *Dead of Night* in 1945], one knew his worth. I didn't know anything about Wills, and I didn't query." Wills's sister, Buntie, was employed behind the scenes on both films, and she is credited as the art director on *Big Fella*. In 1985 Buntie recalled in an interview with the author that her brother, who had died in 1970, had respected Robeson and that during the filming of *Song of Freedom* and *Big Fella* Elisabeth had always arrived at the studio in a chauffeur-driven car, beautifully gowned, with a handsome white man on her arm.

In September 1939, just twenty-four hours after the declaration of war, Elder Wills voluntarily severed his film connections and presented himself for service. He was appointed Head of Sabotage and Camouflage; the wartime experiences of Lieutenant Colonel J. Elder Wills were to be documented in 1957 in Leslie Bell's book *Sabotage*, described as a "fantastic war story of a genius of destruction." After the war, Elder Wills resumed his film career and wrote *Against the Wind* (1948) for Ealing, based on his wartime experiences. He was also appointed a production designer and producer for the Rank Organisation.

In *Song of Freedom* Robeson plays John Zinga, a London-born dock worker who acknowledges Africa as his ancestral home and dreams of visiting it. In a highly improbable and melodramatic plot, he is discovered by Donozetti (Esme Percy), an impresario who transforms him into an internationally acclaimed opera singer. When an anthropologist informs Zinga that he is the direct descendant of an African king, he travels to the west coast of Africa to meet his people, but to his dismay he finds the people of the kingdom are mostly ignorant, superstitious, and poverty-stricken savages. Robeson had tried to act in a film that departed from the traditional racist stereotypes, and had almost succeeded. However, in spite of the film's shortcomings, this production was important to Robeson, because, as he explained in *Film Weekly* (May 23, 1936), he believed it was the first "to give a true picture of many aspects of the life of the coloured man in the west. Hitherto, on the screen, he has been caricatured or presented only as a comedy character. This film shows him as a real man, with problems to be solved, difficulties to be overcome."

Elisabeth's character, Zinga's wife Ruth, is a radical departure from the stereotypical depiction of black women in films up to that time. Neither a mammy, whore, or exotic, she is a well-spoken, warm, and loving wife, but confused and upset about her husband's desire to visit Africa. He tries to explain to her that Africa is "where we come from. What wouldn't I give to know our people? The people we belong to?" But she doesn't understand why her husband wants to leave the comfortable home they have built together, and their close-knit, friendly community, to enter the unknown. Zinga comforts her in a sentimental but touching musical interlude in which he sings a lullaby, "Sleepy River." Said Douglas McVay in *The Musical Film* (1967): "In Britain, the young Paul Robeson . . . makes another haunting song, 'River of Dreams' [*sic*], with the help of tranquil people-at-evening images, a moving flash of film poetry." At the end of this sequence Robeson kisses Elisabeth, probably the first time a black couple were permitted to do so in a film.

On the whole *Song of Freedom* received a favourable reception from critics, but perhaps the most perceptive review came from Britain's Graham Greene in the *Spectator* (September 25, 1936):

> Apart from the profound beauty of Miss Elisabeth Welch and Mr. Robeson's magnificent singing of inferior songs, I find it hard to say in what the charm of this imperfect picture lies. The direction is distinguished but not above reproach, the story is sentimental and absurd, and yet a sense stays in the memory of an unsophisticated mind fumbling on the edge of simple and popular poetry. The best scenes are the dockland scenes, the men returning from work, black and white in an easy companionship free from any colour bar, the public house interiors, dark faces pausing at tenement windows to listen to Zinga's songs, a sense of nostalgia. There are plenty of faults even here, sentiment too close to sentimentality, a touch of "quaintness" and patronage, but one is made aware all the time of what Mann calls "the gnawing surreptitious hankering for the bliss of the commonplace," the general exile of our class as well as the particular exile of the African. But everything goes badly wrong when Zinga reaches Africa. . . . This is not an authentic situation, for the part of Africa untouched by white influence is minute.

One of the most striking features of *Song of Freedom*, and one that has been completely ignored by film historians, is the warm, loving relationship between Zinga and Ruth. Off-screen, Robeson and his co-star admired and respected each other. Art mirrored life in this film, for it reflected Robeson's growing interest in his African heritage and Elisabeth's apolitical stance. Unlike Robeson, Elisabeth was the child of a mixed marriage who distanced herself from politics. However, she had nothing but admiration for Robeson's desire to combat racism:

> It was during the shooting of the film *Song of Freedom* that I got to know—and love—Paul Robeson. Arriving to play opposite that great man—and it being my first speaking part in a film—I was overwhelmed, and as nervous as a kitten. The nerves were soon calmed, however, when I saw that huge smile light up his face, and felt the warmth of a friendly giant when he pressed my hand in both of his, and welcomed me. It was a happy time for me, working with Paul and watching him work. I found him a man of great intensity, both in his work and in his beliefs but—thank goodness—not lacking in humour. We'd sometimes sit outdoors with our lunch trays, chatting about life and living. These were times I can never forget. Often he spoke of his desires and his determination for making a better world and, as often, we argued as to how it could be achieved. Once he tried to persuade me to do something for our people. I had an answer. I'm of mixed blood—African, American Indian, Scots, and Irish. So I said: "Paul, I belong to *four* peoples! I can't make a stand for all of them. You must excuse me!" and he laughed really hard at that. Sometimes there was anger in his voice. There was sadness too. The lunch break over, he'd laugh and say "to be continued tomorrow" and back we'd go to the life and lights of the film studio.

Elisabeth and Robeson attended the premiere of *Song of Freedom*, which took place at the Plaza Cinema at the top of Lower Regent Street, just off Piccadilly Circus. This was the cinema where in 1950 Anna Neagle would attend the Royal Premiere of *Odette*; in 1956 Joan Crawford would be present for a charity premiere of *Autumn Leaves*, almost delaying the start of the film by signing autographs in the street; and where, in 1963, Judy Garland and Dirk Bogarde would attend the world premiere of her final film, *I Could Go On Singing*.

In 1937 Robeson teamed up with Elisabeth again for a charming, lighthearted musical called *Big Fella*, also directed by J. Elder Wills. It was based on the novel *Banjo*, by Claude McKay, a popular Jamaican writer of the Harlem Renaissance. Set in a racially integrated community on the Marseilles waterfront, this uncomplicated tale of a black man who is hired by a wealthy English couple to find their missing son is far removed from *Song of Freedom*. Easy-going and relaxed, Robeson's character, Joe, is quite unlike John Zinga. He's a happy-go-lucky fellow and enjoys taking it easy with his pals, Chuck (James Hayter) and Corney (Lawrence Brown), on the docks. He even sings them a song called "Lazin'." The comedy scenes are nicely played by Robeson and his co-stars. On the waterfront the Café Cosmo is presided over by a beautiful but no-nonsense proprietress, a small role memorably played by Robeson's wife, Eslanda Goode Robeson, also known as "Essie." The proprietress welcomes black and white patrons and employs a racially integrated band to accompany her singer, Manda, played by Elisabeth. She sings two songs, "Harlem in My Heart" and "One Kiss," both of which she recorded commercially. Perhaps the film's most memorable scene is the musical interlude in the Café Cosmo, when Robeson, Elisabeth, and the waterfront community sing "Roll Up, Sailorman." It is one of the most joyful musical sequences of 1930s cinema.

On the set, Elisabeth discovered that Mrs. Robeson was a formidable woman: "Madame was on it. She was rather prissy, like a hospital matron, and she watched Paul like a hawk because everybody loved him, and loved being with him. He loved being with them but she kept people away. It was understandable in a way because he had affairs."

Manda is Joe's sweetheart, and Robeson and Elisabeth are perfectly matched. It is almost impossible to think of another film that depicts a light-hearted romance between a black couple. It is important to acknowledge that Manda is romantically linked to Joe, for it would have been impossible for a Hollywood production of the 1930s to show black characters as anything but asexual, comic servants (think of Hattie McDaniel and Bill Robinson in the Shirley Temple feature *The Little Colonel*, 1935).

Perhaps *Big Fella* is most interesting for the way it allows Manda to be assertive, humorous, and sassy. Manda doesn't refrain from insulting the flirtatious Lorietta (Marcelle Rogez), a white Frenchwoman who is after Joe's money. When she recognises Lorietta at the bar of the Café Cosmo, Manda snaps, "What's wrong with the Monte Video tonight? Have they thrown you out already?" In the 1930s, no black woman in American films would have been permitted to speak to a white woman so directly. In the history of cinema, Manda is a refreshing departure from racial stereotyping.

When *Big Fella* was released in the United States, some critics expressed their dissatisfaction with Robeson for playing what they felt was the stereotyped role of a lazy good-for-nothing. However, other critics showed nothing but enthusiasm for Robeson and *Big Fella*. In Britain, *Film Pictorial* (January 1, 1938) informed its readers, "If you like Paul Robeson's voice (and who doesn't?), you will like *Big Fella*." *Film Weekly* (January 1, 1938) said, "Paul Robeson and Elisabeth Welch sing superbly in a comedy about Marseilles kidnappers. Robeson fans will love it."

Unfortunately, *Big Fella* suffered the fate of Josephine Baker's French films, *Zou Zou* (1934) and *Princess Tam-Tam* (1935)—lack of distribution in the United States and limited availability after the 1930s. For years it was impossible to see *Big Fella*. Biographies of Robeson and studies of his films barely mention this film, and those that do usually dismiss it as lightweight rubbish, not worthy of the great man. This is a shame, for in spite of its faults (low budget, some terrible acting by one or two supporting players), it remains one of the few films to have black stars in romantic leading roles. After years in obscurity, *Big Fella* resurfaced in 1994 at London's National Film Theatre in a retrospective of Elisabeth's film and television career. The screening was well attended, and received a warm reception from the audience, which broke into applause after Robeson had sung "Roll Up, Sailorman." Almost sixty years after it was released, *Big Fella* could still captivate an audience.

In Britain in the mid-1930s Robeson and Elisabeth proved to be an attractive team in the two films they made together. They were perfectly matched in both, and their on-screen partnership should be remembered more often. In 1978 Elisabeth spoke movingly about Robeson in the BBC television documentary *Paul Robeson*. In 1985 her appearance in the Paul Robeson Memorial Concert in London's Queen Elizabeth Hall earned her a standing ovation. Elisabeth held the audience spellbound with her memories of Robeson and performed four songs. They were "Can't Help Lovin' That Man," from *Show Boat*, and "Without a Song," followed by two spirituals, "Sometimes I Feel Like a Motherless Child" and "Swing Low, Sweet Chariot." She also recalled her final meeting with him:

I was appearing in a Christmas show at the Garrick Theatre with Cleo Laine. It was called *Cindy-Ella* and towards the end of the run, in January 1963, after the curtain, one of the stage door people came to my dressing-room. He said "Miss Welch, there's a lady and gentleman to see you." I said: "Who are they?" He said: "I don't know, but his face looks familiar." And I said: "Well, send them in." When he opened the door there was Paul and Essie. They'd come to see me in *Cindy-Ella* and I hadn't seen them for years. He told me he was leaving to go back to America. He took me in his arms and gave me one of his warm, bear-like hugs but something came over me and I thought "this is goodbye" and it was. I never saw him again. He had this intense love of humanity. We all know he fought for years. He gave all his strength, everything he had, until illness hit him and knocked all the force and strength out of him. He was a wonderful person. His humour was so great. I can stand anybody saying anything to me as long as there are smiles and laughter and, my god, when he smiled, the whole world lit up.

Others who took part in the Memorial Concert included Dame Peggy Ashcroft, who read poetry; opera singer Willard White, who sang spirituals; and Paul Robeson, Jr., Afterward, when he thanked Elisabeth for her tribute to his late father, Paul told her that she was "the jewel in the crown" on that memorable evening.

~

CHAPTER SEVEN

Keep the Home Fires Burning

Thank God someone's stopping the show!

When Britain declared war on Germany on September 3, 1939, American citizens were advised by their government to return home, but Elisabeth and Adelaide Hall decided not to go back. They took a great risk, because if Hitler had invaded, they would have been interned. Hundreds of black citizens in Germany "disappeared" during the war, and at least one African American entertainer, Valaida Snow, was imprisoned in a concentration camp by the Nazis in Denmark. Adelaide remained in Britain because she was married to a British subject, the Trinidad-born Bert Hicks, and she refused to leave him. Elisabeth stayed because, she explained, "All my friends were here and I didn't want to leave them."

When war broke out, Elisabeth joined the first concert party to entertain the forces in Britain. The following extract is taken from an unidentified press cutting in her scrapbook dated December 1939:

Nowadays you'll find her not only on British theatre stages, but on the improvised stages of Army and Air Force camps all over the country too. When she's not there, she's probably relaxing in her quiet little flat in a mews. The main room is almost barn-like in its simplicity. It is high, with a raftered ceiling. The walls are completely panelled in oak. A neat writing desk stands right across a huge radiogram. On one side of the fireplace you'd notice a pile of theatre programmes, and on the other a pile of high-brow books. And as near the fire as possible, curled in a deep, soft settee, Elisabeth herself would complete the "furnishings." "I like it here," she laughed, "just by myself. I just sit and read, and I'm quite content, with just Colonel, my fox terrier, to keep me company. When the war broke out, I suppose I could have gone back to the States. I had some good offers, and it may have been a lot safer. But I just felt I'd rather stay here. After all, the British public have given me a wonderful time, in many ways better than the reception I've ever had anywhere else. I feel grateful about that, and if the British people like my stuff, it's up to me to give it to them. Besides, I'm enjoying life better since the war started than at any time. No, don't take that the wrong way. But if you'd been in my place and had some of the audiences I've had, and some of the company which have appeared on the same stages with me, you'd feel proud. There was one concert for a bunch of R.A.F. [Royal Air Force] boys 'somewhere in Britain.' A little hall was packed. Appearing that night were stars like Evelyn Laye, Frances Day and the Western Brothers. Oh, a terrific company. No theatre in the world could afford to hire the lot of us at once. What a crowd! What wonderful appreciation we got! What a thrill we got out of doing it for nothing! We couldn't help having lumps in our throats." And Elisabeth has one very good reason for going back. Her mother is still in America, and worries about how things are going in Britain. She wants her daughter back. But Elisabeth just reassures her . . . and stays.

The German Blitz on London did not start until September 1940, but in the early days of the war, before ENSA (the Entertainments National Service Association) was formed, Elisabeth was happy to join some of her show business friends and entertain the troops:

A lot of artists would call up friends and get parties together, sometimes with War Office permission. If we went out of London, transport was laid on for us. I went to Salisbury a lot. Wherever we went the boys were very pleased to see us. Sometimes they were a bit stunned, agog at who was up there on the stage in front of them—people like Vivien Leigh, Kay Hammond, and Michael Wilding. Often we had no stage. I've been on a truck, with a terrible broken down piano, to sing to about six men on an Ack-Ack site in the middle of nowhere. I don't think they really wanted me to sing—though, as the piano was there, I did—they just wanted somebody to talk to. They were bored, lonely, and tense, waiting for enemy planes to come over.

Throughout the war, in between many stage, film, and radio engagements, Elisabeth kept constantly busy singing to troops and war workers, a job that took her to Royal Air Force hangars, army huts, factories, and workshops all over the country. She toured the provinces many times in variety shows: "I spent a season at Blackpool and many weeks in Bristol when that lovely city was under fire. I played morning shows in Manchester at the Opera House during their terrible Blitz. I was under fire at Portsmouth, Cardiff, Liverpool,

and Leeds, and was in London many times when the place was torn to bits."
Elisabeth also took part in benefits to raise money for various causes. On Sep-
tember 26, 1941, the *Daily Mirror* reported, "Orphan children of London Fire
Service heroes will be helped by an all-star variety concert on Sunday at 3
P.M. at the Piccadilly Theatre, at which over a dozen famous stars are to appear." In addition to Elisabeth, the names listed in the programme included
the cream of British theatre and variety: John Gielgud, Rex Harrison, Roger
Livesey, Ursula Jeans, Noël Coward, Lilli Palmer, Diana Wynyard, Doris
Hare, Emlyn Williams, Edith Evans, Vic Oliver, Tommy Trinder, Flanagan
and Allen, and Debroy Somer's Band. Elisabeth also volunteered her services
for London's popular Stage Door Canteen, which opened in Piccadilly in
1944. A report in the *Daily Express* (April 19, 1945) claimed that Beatrice
Lillie had made more appearances than any other star (twenty-two in just
under a year); Elisabeth was ranked second with "more than 20 appearances
to her credit."

On March 27, 1941, Elisabeth's next West End stage production, *No Time
for Comedy*, opened at the Haymarket Theatre after a successful tour
throughout the provinces and performances for the troops at many camps under the aegis of ENSA. The stars of the London version of S. N. Behrman's
acclaimed Broadway comedy were Rex Harrison, Diana Wynyard, and Lilli
Palmer. Elisabeth played Wynyard's maid Clementine, a departure for the
singer, for this was her first "straight" role in the theatre. Though she played
a maid, Clementine was not the one-dimensional stereotype often seen in
American movies and stage productions at this time. Elisabeth was attracted
to the role because Clementine was as witty and attractive as the rest of the
characters. A review in *The Stage* (April 3, 1941) noted: "Elisabeth Welch
lends vim and force to her vivacious study of Linda's servant." For Elisabeth,
in addition to playing her first non-singing stage role, *No Time for Comedy*
was also memorable for another reason: it opened at the height of the Blitz.

When the air raid sirens went we stopped and whoever was on the stage went
forward and said, "There's an air raid and if anyone wants to leave, please do
so." We had to do this because some people were air raid wardens or ambulance
drivers and had to be on duty. The houselights would come up and we would
hear seats banging as people got up. Then the lights would go down and we
would carry on with the show, praying we wouldn't be hit. In plays they did
that, in the middle of a dramatic scene. When I look back it's strange to remember how everyone kept on working. Every night I wondered if I would still
have a house when I got home. I still have my incendiary bomb shovel, I kept
it as a souvenir.

After a long break from West End musicals, Elisabeth returned in the revue *Sky High*, which opened at the Phoenix Theatre on June 4, 1942, and co-starred Hermione Gingold and Hermione Baddeley. True to form, she stopped the show: "My hit number in that was 'Europa' which I sang sitting on a big prop bull!" In 1985 Baddeley recalled for Elisabeth's *This Is Your Life* tribute on British television, "I remember the opening night of *Sky High* very well indeed. Hermione Gingold was with me, and this [Elisabeth] comes on, looking superb, and of course she was singing this great song 'Europa' magnificently. Well, of course, stand up ovation and Gingold was fishing as the mermaid and she said to me, 'We should have better material.' I said, 'Shut up! Thank God someone's stopping the show!' She went on stopping the show and many others."

In the summer of 1943 Elisabeth enjoyed another season at the Blackpool Opera House in the revue *We're All in It*, joining a cast that included Wilfred Pickles and the popular comedy duo Jimmy Jewell and Ben Warris. On November 9, 1943, she opened at the Phoenix Theatre in Ivor Novello's *Arc de Triomphe* with Mary Ellis: "I played a French cabaret singer called Josie, all feathers, jewels, and sequins, who was based on Josephine Baker. I sang 'Dark Music' on a barge lit by fairy lamps on the River Seine in Paris. Peter Graves was Mary's leading man because Ivor was still in *The Dancing Years* at the Adelphi." *Arc de Triomphe* spanned the years 1906 to 1925; it was a backstage story of young love and operatic success through the war years in Paris. Ellis concluded the evening as Jeanne d'Arc in an operatic excerpt. It was not one of Novello's most successful ventures. Said Derek and Julia Parker in *The Story and the Song: A Survey of English Musical Plays 1916–78* (1979),

> It had several limitations, one of which was that Ivor himself did not appear in it. There were a couple of good numbers—"Paris Reminds Me of You," which Peter Graves sang and danced, and a quieter number, "Dark Music," sung by Elisabeth Welch. But it is badly constructed (the hero is dead before the evening is half over), and the lack of spectacular effects was no help. The final blow to the show was the bad publicity when Ivor, in April 1944, was sentenced to eight weeks' imprisonment for a petty infringement of the Motor Vehicles Order restricting the use of petrol for private purposes during the war.

Next came one of Elisabeth's most popular stage successes, *Happy and Glorious*. Opening at the London Palladium on October 3, 1944, it ran for a record-breaking 938 performances until May 1946: "I was so happy working with Tommy Trinder in *Happy and Glorious* at the Palladium. Two shows a day. We were in the theatre about half past eleven in the morning and we got out about seven at night. It was a big revue, very glamorous with lovely dancing girls, two of whom were the sisters Kay and Kim Kendall. We were in the midst of another Blitz. This time Hitler was sending over the V-2 rockets, and we just had to cope." Tommy Trinder, whose famous catchphrase was "You lucky people," was later reunited with Elisabeth in her *This Is Your Life* tribute. He said: "You made a lot of audiences feel that they were very lucky people. I'm in a show at the Palladium with this wonderful lady and there wasn't a night went past, when she was on her way home, when she'd say, 'Good night, Honey Chile!' and I used to say, 'Good night, Colonel!' That was her dog and he used to bark at me."

In December 1941 America entered the war, and Elisabeth was more than happy to sing for American troops stationed in Britain. A report in the *Performer* (April 29, 1943) described an appearance she made for the American Red Cross:

> The American Red Cross certainly gave the boys from the U.S.A. a treat on Easter Monday when Dwight Deere Wiman, the Broadway producer, put on a first-class show in the theatre at the Rainbow Corner (on the site of the old Lyon's) in Shaftesbury Avenue. The all-star programme included Beatrice Lillie, Edythe Baker, Adele Astaire, Michael Wilding, Elisabeth Welch, and Douglas Byng, supported by the G.I. (Government Issue—Enlisted Men) talent. The show, a great success, is the forerunner of others to come.

However, black troops stationed in Britain suffered appalling discrimination, but though she objected to them being segregated, Elisabeth welcomed opportunities to sing to the black members of the American forces, as reported by Hannen Swaffer in the *Daily Herald* (September 16, 1942): "Already Ben Lyon and his associates—who in their spare time are running ENSA for the United States troops—have arranged special concerts for the coloured soldiers at which only Negroes—Turner Layton, Adelaide Hall, Scott and Whaley and Elisabeth Welch—perform. Sometimes the audience contains as many as 3000 black troops!" During the war, on BBC radio, Elisabeth was featured in several overseas broadcasts for the Caribbean. These included *West Indian Party* (1941), in which she sang "The Nearness of You" and "The London I Love," and *Calling the West Indies* (1941).

In November 1942 Elisabeth was appearing in Manchester when a telegram arrived from the War Office asking if she would travel to Gibraltar to entertain the garrison there in *Christmas Party*, an all-star revue. The company flew out to Gibraltar on December 23, 1942:

> Well, what greater compliment could be asked of a foreigner than to join the company of people like Phyllis Stanley, Jeanne de Casalis, Dame Edith Evans, Beatrice Lillie, John Gielgud, and Michael Wilding? I was very proud, and

grateful! We were asked by the War Office to go out to Gibraltar to entertain the troops. Not ENSA, but HM [His Majesty's] Government itself, the men with red braid on their caps. I felt very grand. We flew out in a Dutch plane with the windows all blacked out because we weren't supposed to see where we were going. We landed in Lisbon in what looked like a sea of swastikas. Because Portugal was neutral everyone stopped there for repairs and refuelling, and it was quite a shock to step out of the plane and see Nazi planes all round us. We girls gave our own brasshats a shock too. We were all three wearing trousers and they asked us frostily to change, which we did not.

Only Gordon Marsh's *Swingtime Follies* and one other ENSA show had visited Gibraltar before them. *Christmas Party* had been organised by Hugh "Binkie" Beaumont of H. M. Tennant's, a management that made sure its stars played troop shows:

Well, we began rehearsing for the first show, and John [Gielgud] had been given a poem to read. It was a tribute to the men who were fighting for us and John got into a funk about it. He's a shy man, and he said, "How can I go out and recite something about fighting for our country when we're not in uniform and we'll be flown back to London and looked after and lauded? How can I stand in front of these men?" I told John, don't worry, I'd sing something to set the scene. So I began to sing Noël Coward's "London Pride" quietly behind the curtains to get the boys into the mood. Then he spoke these words, and you could hear a pin drop. They were very emotional days, especially out there in Gibraltar where the boys were going to be killed and the ships to be sunk. It's hard to sing when your throat tightens up and you are fighting back tears, but for an actor it's different, and John has always had a little nervy thing, an emotional sort of timbre to his voice.

During their four-week stay the company performed fifty-six shows, including one on board ship to more than two thousand men, two in the local hospitals, and some on board battleships and aircraft carriers. They also toured gun-sites, where they talked to the men. Most of the shows were given in the island's Rock Theatre. Said Richard Fawkes in *Fighting for a Laugh: Entertaining the British and American Armed Forces 1939–1946* (1978):

When the curtains opened on the first performance, Edith Evans, dressed in the costume Oliver Messel had designed for her as Millament in *The Way of the World*, stood ready to recite a poem written especially for the occasion. The audience, most of whom had no idea what they were about to see, thought, since it was Christmas, it was a pantomime. They began to laugh. Dame Edith stood her ground until they fell silent then started to recite. As the words died away, the men exploded into applause, half in apology for their rudeness earlier, half because they realized they were in the presence of a great artist.

The island's Rock Theatre held about 750 people. It was packed at every performance, officers and men all sitting together, which created a better atmosphere than in the English camps, where they were always separated. Most of the troops had been stationed in Gibraltar for two years and were having a very dull time, so they were a responsive and grateful audience. There were two performances every night, including Sundays. Following Edith Evans's opening appearance Elisabeth took the stage. It was a memorable performance, briefly described by Gielgud in the May 1943 edition of *Theatre Arts:* "Elisabeth Welch sings 'Prayer for Rain,' 'Begin the Beguine,' and 'Solomon,' in a black dress against a white satin curtain, and you can hear a pin drop while she is singing, but when she has finished the thunder of applause can be heard in the street."

One of Elisabeth's most memorable wartime experiences was an invitation to sing to some Scottish troops on New Year's Eve, 1942:

After my two shows at the Garrison theatre in Gibraltar, I was asked to sing to some Scottish troops up in a castle in the hills—after which I was to rejoin Gielgud's troupe at a party at Government House. The drive to the castle was along very narrow winding roads. It was pitch black, but the sky was brilliant with stars. Then out of the darkness came the music of Cole Porter's "Begin the Beguine." Someone was playing a record—I couldn't see where it came from—but there it was. How weird, I thought, but how right—and we soon passed into quietness again. I got to the castle all right, but I never got to sing because the boys were, shall we say, in *very* high spirits! Well, if you know Scotland or the Scots on New Year's Eve, you'll know what Hogmanay means to them. Being half Scots myself, I wanted to join in the Revelry—but instead I found myself being driven back down the hill to Government House where, funnily enough, as I entered—the band was playing "Begin the Beguine." After about five hours after curfew, I got back to my room at the hotel, and there—I couldn't believe my eyes—my bed was covered with flowers! I thought, "Welch, you're dreaming," but I pinched myself and I wasn't. I found a card. It was from the boys up at the castle. They'd heard I'd come up to sing, and so I wouldn't feel disappointed, they sent me down all these flowers! I sat down and cried and, looking out from my balcony windows, I saw again that purple star-studded sky and palm trees and I thought the music for this little episode was well chosen, for here was the real setting to Cole Porter's "Begin the Beguine."

After the war, Elisabeth's war service was to be overlooked. Though she stayed in Britain for the duration and worked hard for the war effort, there was no formal recognition. In 1939 she could have returned to New York, but Elisabeth remained loyal to her adopted king and country, and put herself at risk. Regrettably, she was not awarded an OBE (Officer of the Order of the British Empire) or CBE (Commander of the Order of the British Empire) in the Honours Lists.

John Gielgud's company returned to England on January 22, 1943, but four years later Elisabeth readily agreed to go back to Gibraltar with another concert party, in March 1947. They were scheduled to give performances for troops under the auspices of Combined Services Entertainments, but they failed to arrive, having crash-landed near Cadiz:

Kay Cavendish, Richard Hearne, Douglas Byng, and I took off from Croydon in a tiny airplane early one cold Sunday morning. Some hours later we were flying very low among some very sharp-looking Spanish mountains in a terrible storm. The radio was out of action, the rain was pouring in on us, our petrol was running low, and we were lost. At last we saw a bit of green below and the pilot decided we'd better try and make a landing. So we braced ourselves for a bang, but instead of that it was a dull plonk and we sank in mud up to the wing-spread. Out we climbed on to the wing, green with fright, wet and very bedraggled. No wonder the locals stared. They'd struggled through the rain and mud up to our plane, but just stood staring. Not one of us knew a word of Spanish, so a series of miming, pidgin French and Spanish began. Finally we were taken through mud up to our knees to a little house where we were put around a table near a roaring fire. Joy of joys, there was also a charcoal burner under the table to warm our legs and a lot of children running about. They were very poor people, but offered us food, which we refused, but we had some hot water and some wine to warm us. We somehow made them understand we were artists, so of course they asked us to perform, which somehow we did. Then someone brought in a guitar, and they proceeded to entertain us with their wonderful flamenco singing and playing. They bedded us down late that night on straw on the floor of that little house, but who could sleep after so much excitement? Richard Hearne and our pilot, Douglas Neill, waded three rivers to get to a phone. Exhausted, they sent an SOS to the British Consul at Cadiz. We were eventually rescued by a mule team, but we stayed with the villagers long enough to get to enjoy flamenco singing. We rode two-to-a-mule to Algar whose 1500 strong population thronged to the main street to greet us. After drying out, we were treated to a huge banquet.

During the war Elisabeth's film career continued with *This Was Paris* (1942). Originally titled *You Can't Escape Forever*, it was directed by John Harlow and filmed at Warner Brothers' Teddington Studios. Set in Paris in 1940, this entertaining espionage adventure starred Griffith Jones as a British intelligence officer and Ann Dvorak as the French dress designer (and fifth columnist) he falls for. Dvorak was a Hollywood actress who spent the war in Britain while her husband served in the Royal Navy. Elisabeth made a brief but striking appearance as a cabaret singer and performed "All This and Heaven Too." During the filming she told a reporter for *Picture Show* (July 12, 1941) that the song had been originally intended for—but not used in—another Warner Brothers film, also called *All This and Heaven Too*, starring Bette Davis and Charles Boyer. For the first—and last—time in her screen career, Elisabeth's name was omitted from the opening and closing credits.

Also in 1942, the British film director Brian Desmond Hurst featured Elisabeth as another Parisian cabaret entertainer—this time with a screen credit—in the crime thriller *Alibi*, starring Margaret Lockwood and James Mason. The story was set in Paris in 1937; Lockwood played a night club hostess who helps an inspector to trap a murderous mind-reader. Elisabeth sang two numbers, including the lovely "Chez Moi" with music by Paul Misraki and English words by Bruce Sievier, from the French of Jean Feline. The May 15, 1942, edition *To-Day's Cinema* reported: "Over 200 dancers are seen in one of the big scenes in *Alibi*, a tremendous setting, with bright lights and gay music, realistically representative of gay, pre-war Paris. For these scenes, Clarie Wear's Rhumba Band was engaged, as was also the famous coloured singer Elisabeth Welch."

Elisabeth was a neighbour of Brian Desmond Hurst's, and he claimed to be a cousin of the Hollywood director John "Jack" Ford. During the war, Ford was a naval commander in charge of filming for the psychological warfare unit. Hurst invited him to stay at his home in Kinnerton Street and one night gave a party for his "cousin." It was, according to Hurst in his unpublished autobiography, *Travelling the Road*, "attended by every important person in the American and British film industry in London at the time. A bomb could have blown away a lot of very talented filmmakers." The guests included Hermione Gingold, also a Kinnerton Street neighbour, with some of the chorus boys from one of her stage revues. Elisabeth was sitting on a large sofa at the end of the room, surrounded by some of the chorus boys. Says Hurst: "Jack looked across at her and asked, 'Who is that beautiful coloured girl up to her arse in pansies?'" Elisabeth enjoyed the company of neighbours like Hurst and Gingold:

I met Brian some years before we made *Alibi*. He gave fantastic parties and everybody came. Everybody knew Brian as a director who was very important in the film world. He lived in a private mews in a beautiful studio which had a gallery all round the inside. He always had plenty of money. Brian and

Hermione were lovely people and, in 1959, when I had to leave Cottage Walk, they persuaded me to move into a flat in Capener's Close, a small mews situated off Kinnerton Street. It wasn't very far from my home in Cottage Walk. That's how we became proper neighbours. It was a well-known and very exclusive artist's residential section of Belgravia. Many big names lived in the area. We had pianists, musicians, painters—a real "colony" of creative, elegant people. I suppose you could say it was the Greenwich Village of London! A lot of people envied us. It was a wonderful place to live—secluded, respectable, but fun.

Though Elisabeth was discreet about her friends' private lives and never publicly referred to Hurst's sexual exploits, his promiscuous gay lifestyle was common knowledge in the film world. He once described himself as "trisexual" ("the Army, the Navy, and the household cavalry"). Journalist Patrick Newley once described Hurst to the author as "a great character and full of energy (both mental and other) well up until he was ninety odd. If you managed to stop him talking about sailors and soldiers, and who was on the game, he was dazzlingly knowledgeable about the film business and the early days of Hollywood, and had a keen insight to the role of film making."

Towards the end of the war, Elisabeth made appearances in two Ealing films: *Fiddlers Three* (1944) and *Dead of Night* (1945). In *Fiddlers Three*, directed by Harry Watt, comedian Tommy Trinder played a soldier who is transported back in time to ancient Rome while taking shelter from a thunderstorm at Stonehenge. It's a daft musical comedy but contains some bright moments, recalling Eddie Cantor's Hollywood musical *Roman Scandals* (1933). Elisabeth is featured in the supporting cast as Thora, a beautiful and exotic handmaiden to Nero's wife Poppae (Frances Day). She shares several comedy scenes with Trinder, which are a delight, but, disappointingly, she has only one song to sing, "Drums in My Heart," performed at Nero's orgy. For the first and only time in her film career Elisabeth portrayed a servant, but the actress disregards her character's station in life and just has fun playing herself—warm and witty. These were the qualities she brought to her next role, Beulah, in *Dead of Night*. This film classic includes five supernatural tales, and it is most famous for the powerful and chilling segment called "The Ventriloquist's Dummy," directed by Alberto Cavalcanti. It is arguably Cavalcanti's most famous work, and the segment is the film's most celebrated.

Michael Redgrave took the lead role as Maxwell Frere, an unhappy, tortured ventriloquist who, with his doll Hugo Fitch, is the star attraction at the Chez Beulah, a classy nightclub in pre-war Paris. The club is owned by a glamorous, friendly African American expatriate; for the first time in a film, a black woman is portrayed as independent, successful, and resourceful. In spite of her name—which conjures up an image of a Hollywood mammy— Beulah serves customers, not a white mistress. Though not a very big part, nevertheless it is significant, as Peter Noble pointed out in his book *The Negro in Films* (1948): "Here she [Elisabeth Welch] acted as the popular Parisian nightclub owner who sang the blues, joked with the customers, was a good friend to everyone and was altogether an attractive personality. She played an important part in the development of the plot, and was featured in the film's billing with such eminent players as Michael Redgrave, Googie Withers, Mervyn Johns and Frederick Valk."

Like Ruth Zinga and Manda in the two Robeson films of the 1930s, Elisabeth's role in *Dead of Night* was a breakthrough in the portrayal of black women in films. In Hollywood in 1945, Elisabeth's contemporary, Lena Horne, who was then under contract to MGM, was not allowed to appear on screen with white actors or musicians. Under pressure from distributors in the racially segregated southern states, MGM was even forced to cut Horne out of its films before they were shown to southern film-goers. This was not the case in Britain with Elisabeth in *Dead of Night*. In addition to playing important scenes with white actors, as a character who was their equal, she performed a number, "The Hullalooba," with white musicians (Frank Weir and his Sextet). *Dead of Night* also hints at something unheard of in films at that time. When Sylvester Kee (Hartley Power), a white American ventriloquist, visits the Chez Beulah, he is reunited with Beulah, an old friend from New York. He greets her with "Eh, you old warhorse, you look terrific. Just like the lights of Broadway on a dark night." The couple flirt a little, and their intimacy suggests that they may have had a relationship.

Though easily missed, this is nonetheless the closest any English-language film had come to suggesting a racially mixed relationship between a woman of African descent and a white man. Strict censorship in Hollywood prohibited any depiction of this until 1957, when Harry Belafonte and Dorothy Dandridge played West Indians with white lovers in *Island in the Sun*— though the two couples were not allowed to kiss on the screen. In Britain a mixed-race relationship was finally depicted on the screen in *Flame in the Streets* (1961), a melodrama that starred Sylvia Syms as a school teacher who announces to her family that she intends to marry a Jamaican colleague (Johnny Sekka).

In spite of her excellent work in *Dead of Night*, Elisabeth was not offered an important film role for more than thirty years, when Derek Jarman cast her as a "Goddess" in his film of William Shakespeare's *The Tempest* (1979) (see chapter 9). If you blinked you missed her in *Our Man in Havana* (1960),

Girl Stroke Boy (1971), *Revenge of the Pink Panther* (1978), and *Arabian Adventure* (1979). There was a featured role in the aborted version of *Cleopatra* (1960) (see chapter 8), but until Jarman rediscovered her for the movies, there was only one appearance of consequence. In 1946 Elisabeth participated in a BBC demonstration film called *Television Is Here Again*, in which she sang a medley of "St. Louis Blues" and "Stormy Weather," accompanied by Debroy Somers and his Orchestra. The film celebrated the post-war resumption of the BBC's television broadcasts (in June 1946), and it was mainly used in demonstrating and installing sets. It was also shown as a support feature in cinemas.

CHAPTER EIGHT

~

A Marvellous Party

An *artiste* of brilliant versatility

After the war, Elisabeth reigned supreme in London's West End in three so-phisticated revues devised and directed by Laurier Lister: *Tuppence Coloured* (1947), *Oranges and Lemons* (1948), and *Penny Plain* (1951). Each of them gave her opportunities to shine as an *artiste* and, true to form, in each pro-duction, Elisabeth stopped the show.

In *Tuppence Coloured*, which opened at the Lyric Theatre in Hammer-smith on September 4, 1947, and transferred to the Globe Theatre the fol-lowing month, Elisabeth co-starred with Joyce Grenfell and Max Adrian and introduced to Britain a song she had "discovered" in Paris:

> Right after the war, in October 1946, I went over to Paris to look up some friends, and it was there that I first heard this name, Edith Piaf. Everyone was talking about her and she was playing at a wonderful theatre called the Olympia, an enormous house, so I went to see her. I'll never forget that evening. This little waif appeared on the stage and walked to the centre. There was no glamour, or beauty, but when she opened her mouth you were ab-solutely fascinated by the passion and the force that came out of this woman. She was so fantastic. Then she sang *"La Vie en Rose."* She was a person who loved to be in love, and that year she was in love and so she wrote the lyric to this song. I saw her again one night in a little club on the Left Bank but I never met her. I found a copy of *"La Vie en Rose,"* and brought it to London but I had no place to sing it. The following year Laurier Lister started his series of revues

with *Tuppence Coloured*. When we were putting it together I submitted some songs, threw a few music sheets on the floor for Laurier to look at, and he said "What's that over there?" He'd seen Piaf's face on one of the music sheets. I said "I can't do that because it's French" and he said "Why not?" So we put it in the show but I said if I sing it, I sing it in French because when they make translations they're diabolical. *Tuppence Coloured* was a big success and every-where I sang *"La Vie en Rose,"* on tour in places like Aberdeen and Liverpool, and then in London, it had a fantastic reception. It's a beautiful song, even if you don't know French. I love the song because it's from the heart, and Piaf sang it from the heart. I'm so proud I introduced it to Britain.

In *Tuppence Coloured* Elisabeth introduced another song to Britain, Irving Berlin's "Supper Time." This had been introduced by Ethel Waters in 1933 in Berlin's Broadway revue *As Thousands Cheer*. It told the story of an African American woman who is feeding her children, waiting for her husband to come home, not knowing he has been lynched. This song marked a dramatic change for Elisabeth, but somehow it did not come off, as her friend, Michael Alexander, recalls: "Irving Berlin's 'Supper Time' was a major departure for Elisabeth. She was dressed like a poor Southern woman in a kitchen but she was not allowed to perform the song as starkly as Ethel Waters did, so it did not make a big impact, but she did the Jean-Paul Sartre number, 'Sartre Resartus,' wonderfully, and brought the house down." In "Sartre Resartus" Elisabeth poked fun at Jean-Paul Sartre's plays *Men without Shadows* and *The Respectable Prostitute*, which had preceded *Tuppence Coloured* at the Lyric.

Elisabeth's reviews for *Tuppence Coloured* were outstanding, and in her scrapbook they stand as a testament to her artistry and on-stage brilliance: "Miss Welch is full of vitality and versatility, the range between her satire on Sartre and Irving Berlin's 'Supper Time' being very wide" (*Daily Telegraph*); "Particularly emerges as an artiste of brilliant versatility" (*Theatre World*); "Sings with her customary exquisite artistry and also reveals a grand gift of comedy" (*Jewish Chronicle*); "The pick of the evening is Elisabeth Welch's 'Sartre Resartus,' a lively, not to say brilliant, comment on the philosophy ex-pounded in the Lyric's preceding productions" (*Queen*); "But the singing by Elisabeth Welch of 'Beasts of Prey' and 'Supper Time,' which was not funny at all, stands out for me as the most memorable experience of a memorable evening" (*Advertisers Weekly*); "As for Elisabeth Welch, she is an enchant-ment, and turns the dear little Lyric into a real Parisian *boîte*. No micro-phone, no display—just witty words or telling sentiment, a good tune and rest, all technique, personality and attack" (*Time and Tide*); "Is at her best and gets her songs over in that way of hers that makes every individual member of the audience think she is singing direct at them" (*Playgoer*).

Oranges and Lemons opened at the Lyric Theatre in Hammersmith on November 26, 1948, and transferred to the Globe in January 1949. Once again Elisabeth co-starred with Max Adrian, but Grenfell was replaced with Diana Churchill. Elisabeth impressed the critics with several solo numbers, including "The Spanish Lady," with lyric by Clemence Dane and music by Richard Addinsell, and "Just across the Way." A highlight was "Snake in the Grass," which she performed with Max Adrian. *Oranges and Lemons* was described in the *Daily Times* (November 27, 1948) as "spiritually at any rate, the second edition of *Tuppence Coloured:* one good *revue* is very apt to beget another. It is not perhaps so witty as its predecessor, but it is no less sprightly, no less tuneful, no less pretty and cheering; it finds its mildly satirical targets here, there and everywhere, and it is decidedly stronger in spectacle."

Both *Oranges and Lemons* (on May 14, 1949) and *Tuppence Coloured* (on August 26, 1949) were adapted for BBC television and transmitted live from Alexandra Palace with their original casts.

A private person, Elisabeth seldom gave interviews to the press, but she did consent to being profiled at the height of the favourable publicity generated by her appearances in post-war revues. In *SW3* (September 25, 1948), J. Pardoe offered readers an insight into her personality and private life:

> Elisabeth Welch's personality is a harmonious one, tuned to the triad of generosity, charm and sparkle. Whoever heard her deep genuine laugh will recognise it as the expression of a generous mind that gives freely, and gladly lets others partake of the gifts which nature gave her. Vivacity, grace and intelligent facility of conversation as well as a gift for listening when her interest is roused, predestine her as the centre of every party. Her exquisitely feminine ways, her chic and elegant appearance, her sparkling yet never adder-sharp wit form a piquant contrast to the childlike, credulous streak which is also part of her mental makeup. She quickly sums up people and has a good insight into human nature. . . . Elisabeth loves to entertain her numerous friends. She loves her home to which she always returns with a deep sigh of contentment—be it from touring or travelling for pleasure's sake. She likes travelling and has just come back from a holiday in Copenhagen where she particularly enjoyed visiting the picture galleries. Her interests are manifold, comprising the spheres of belles-lettres and the arts. She is a reader of discrimination. . . . Miss Welch is an excellent cook and spends many a night after the theatre working in her cosy kitchen. She turns out delicious pastry with almost professional proficiency and speed and in great variety. It is one way of relaxation she says. Another way of relaxing used to be a midnight walk with "Colonel"—"the

Colonel" as he was called by his mistress. This wire-haired terrier was a well-known character in the neighbourhood and a friend of all her friends. His death about a year ago broke up such a companionship that no successor has so far been thought of. . . . Elisabeth Welch is a staunch friend to her friends, a most loyal and helpful colleague, a gay and ever stimulating companion, but she doesn't like to meet people whom she doesn't like—she says.

Joyce Grenfell came back with Elisabeth and Max Adrian for another hit revue, *Penny Plain*, which opened at the St. Martin's Theatre on June 28, 1951. This gentle, charming entertainment also featured Desmond Walter-Ellis, Rose Hill, Moyra Fraser, and June Whitfield. Geoffrey Tarran in *Morning Advertiser* (August 24, 1951) enthused: "With her honeyed tones and captivating mannerisms Miss Welch can work wonders with the poorest song but in this revue she has several very satisfactory ones. Homely pleasures are enticingly stressed in 'Festival Calypso' and another diverting re-statement of the Godiva theme ['Good Day for Godiva'] leads to strong encouragement for modern women to take a leaf out of her book to bring about lower taxes. Just before the end, Miss Welch sings about tours among the little food shops of Paris ['The Patisserie'] and she conveys an enchanting picture of French domesticity." Press reports—and an entry in Elisabeth's diary—testify that on December 13, 1951, Queen Elizabeth and Princess Margaret attended a performance of *Penny Plain* and afterwards met the cast. "Heavy fog" kept King George VI indoors. A few weeks later, on February 6, he passed away. On March 15, 1952, the *Star* noted that "tonight's performance of *Penny Plain* is the 300th. None of the principals has missed a single performance."

Joyce Grenfell later recalled the successful provincial tours of *Tuppence Coloured* and *Penny Plain* in her autobiography, *Joyce Grenfell Requests the Pleasure* (1976):

> Touring after a run in London could not only be financially rewarding but also pleasant, and, because of the good company of Elisabeth Welch, Max Adrian and others in the cast, I enjoyed the tours that followed both revues. Lis, Max and I usually stayed in the same hotel and spent our evenings together after the performance. We supped and sat up late talking in the colossal public rooms of most of the station hotels in the north, and I remember creeping along the high endless corridors of the Midland, Manchester, and the Central, Glasgow, on our way to bed, amusing ourselves by rearranging the shoes left outside bedroom doors to be cleaned. . . . We never muddled up the shoes, we simply put them in new positions *in situ*—toes turned in or out; one toe on top of the next; boots wide apart or going in opposite directions; up-ended on their toes—the variations were infinite. We competed to discover new ways of arranging them and found the silly game remarkably diverting. All of us were sober.

In 1949 Elisabeth began her long association with all-star charity and fund-raising galas. On November 20, at the Coliseum in Covent Garden, she sang "Solomon" in *Merely Players*. This star-studded affair, devised by Diana Morgan, was organised by the committee of Equity's projected social club to raise money for the club's equipment fund. A review in *The Stage* (November 24, 1949) described the event as "something like an abbreviated edition of *Who's Who in the Theatre*." Elisabeth joined an extraordinary cast that included Edith Evans, Dolores Gray, Peggy Ashcroft, Paul Scofield, Kay Hammond, John Clements, Jessie Matthews, John Mills, Felix Aylmer, Mary Clare, Sybil Thorndike, Lewis Casson, Stanley Holloway, Alicia Markova, Anton Dolin, and Ralph Richardson.

On February 4, 1951, at the Theatre Royal, Drury Lane, Elisabeth took part in another all-star edition of *Merely Players*, this time in aid of six theatrical charities. The sudden death of Charles B. Cochran on January 30 lent a special poignancy to the occasion. To honour his memory the production included "A Cochran Revue" with Elisabeth and Jessie Matthews. Others in the cast included Evelyn Laye, Lizbeth Webb, Robert Morley (as Oscar Wilde), Emlyn Williams (as Charles Dickens), Anna Neagle (as Queen Victoria), Eric Portman, Marie Burke, and Judy Campbell.

Later that year, the passing of Ivor Novello, another British theatre legend associated with Elisabeth, led to an emotionally charged star-studded charity gala, *Salute to Ivor Novello*, at the Coliseum on October 7. Novello, who had died on March 6 aged just fifty-eight, was one of the best-liked and most respected men in British theatre. Mary Ellis, Noël Coward, Ralph Richardson, Edith Evans, John Gielgud, Richard Attenborough, Jack Buchanan, Beatrice Lillie, and Richard Burton were just a few of the many glittering stars on stage that evening. To bring down the interval curtain, Gracie Fields, accompanied by the band of H.M. Welsh Guards, sang "Keep the Home Fires Burning." Elisabeth sang "Far Away in Shanty Town."

On March 30, 1952, at Drury Lane, Elisabeth performed Noël Coward's "Twentieth Century Blues" in another edition of *Merely Players*, and on June 24, 1954, she performed "Solomon" in *Night of 100 Stars* at the London Palladium, a charity revue in aid of the Actors' Orphanage. Organised by Noël Coward, the cast also included Evelyn Laye, Joyce Grenfell, and Laurence Olivier.

Another Laurier Lister revue, *Pay the Piper*, opened at the Saville Theatre on December 21, 1954, but it was not a success. Said Elisabeth: "We toured it for months trying to make the thing work. It was Elsie and Doris Waters' debut in revue. They were marvellous people and we had great fun working together. After all the hard work we arrived at the Saville just before Christmas and closed about three weeks later."

With no Grenfell or Adrian in the cast, Elisabeth found herself sharing the stage with Elsie and Doris Waters, whose material was better suited to music hall than West End revue. Says Michael Alexander:

> Elsie and Doris were popular in music halls and on the radio, but they were not the draw they were expected to be. They were upset on the opening night because Elisabeth stopped the show twice with Rodgers and Hart's "To Keep My Love Alive," sitting on a throne, and Johnny Ray's "Such a Night" which, earlier in the year, had gone to number one in the British charts. The audience would not stop applauding after "Such a Night," even after Elisabeth had left the stage. So Elsie and Doris, who had followed her on stage, had to go off and come on again. Elisabeth was embarrassed.

The revues in which Elisabeth starred during 1947–54 extended her range as a performer, but throughout her career, Elisabeth made only occasional appearances in straight, dramatic roles. There were few openings for black actresses in Britain, but she fared better than most. In addition to the film *Song of Freedom* (1936) (see chapter 6), for BBC radio, Elisabeth acted in George Bernard Shaw's *The Adventures of the Black Girl in Her Search for God* (1944), Alan Paton's *Cry, the Beloved Country* (1955), and a couple of plays by black dramatists: Jamaica's Sylvia Wynter (*Under the Sun*, 1958, in which she costarred with Cleo Laine) and America's Alice Childress (*Trouble in Mind*, 1964, part of the BBC's ambitious *Negro in America* series).

On television Elisabeth acted in several plays, including adaptations of S. N. Behrman's *No Time for Comedy* (BBC, 1954) and Truman Capote's whimsical *The Grass Harp* (ITV, 1957). Of the latter, Peter Black in the *Daily Mail* (December 12, 1957) said: "It was notable for the striking performance from Elisabeth Welch full of intelligence, strength, and sense of character. I wish I could think of better parts for her. It is absurd that such a talent and a face to set a painter's fingers itching should not be seen more often." In 1956 the BBC cast her opposite Eartha Kitt in an ambitious version of Kitt's Broadway success *Mrs. Patterson*. Kitt played an adolescent daydreamer living in America's Deep South of the 1920s. Elisabeth was cast as a blues singer, Bessie Bolt. This live transmission, screened in the popular *Sunday-Night Theatre* slot on June 17, was the first BBC production to be televised from the new Riverside Studios in Hammersmith. It was a demanding role for Kitt, who was on camera for almost the entire seventy-five minutes. In 1988, when a telerecording of this unusual production was located by the author in the National Film and Television Archive, a private screening was organised for Elisabeth. Memories came flooding back about her old friend, Connie Smith, and an incident involving Miss Kitt.

Born in New York in 1875, Connie Smith had settled in Britain in the 1890s and spent many years treading the boards, first as a music hall entertainer, then as a character actress. In 1928 she understudied Alberta Hunter in the Drury Lane production of *Show Boat* and in 1936 played a small role in the prologue to the film *Song of Freedom*. Elisabeth worked with Connie on several occasions, mostly radio, including a variety show called *Molasses Club* (1936) and the play *Broadway Slave* (1944), in which they portrayed mother and daughter. Elisabeth, who was very fond of Connie, was quite unprepared for what happened at the rehearsals for *Mrs. Patterson*:

> Eartha Kitt was a strange creature. During rehearsals she didn't socialise with any of the cast and one day she upset me. Connie was beginning to lose her sight and had trouble remembering her lines. She needed the job. She didn't have many opportunities to work at her age, but Madame had her thrown off *Mrs. Patterson*. It must have been deeply humiliating for Connie. I was furious and never forgave Eartha Kitt for that. Now and again I noticed Eartha reading a huge book in the Green Room. When she wasn't around, I picked up the book, to find out what it was called. It was a biography of Winston Churchill, but when I opened it several five pound notes fell to the floor! As I bent over to pick them up, and replace them in the book, Eartha walked into the room and gave me such a look of horror. Deeply embarrassed, I stuffed the notes back into the book, and said something about "You should put this money in a bank account or it may be stolen."

Happily for Connie Smith, who died in 1970 at the age of ninety-five, the incident did not affect her career. She continued acting in the theatre and on television until her retirement in the 1960s. When she became a member of the English Stage Company at the Royal Court in 1956, she came close to being reunited with Elisabeth in one of their productions, *The Member of the Wedding*.

A diary entry for November 30, 1956, confirms that Elisabeth attended a reading, at the Lyric Theatre in Shaftesbury Avenue, for the first London production of Carson McCullers's play adapted from her novel *The Member of the Wedding*. It was to be directed by Tony Richardson, who after a brief time at the BBC had become one of the most influential forces in British theatre. In 1956 he joined the English Stage Company at the Royal Court Theatre. McCullers's novel was published in 1946 and formed the basis for her critically acclaimed 1950 Broadway play and the subsequent 1952 film starring Ethel Waters and Julie Harris (who was Oscar nominated). Harris played Frankie, a motherless adolescent in the American South, who survives her awkward and sometimes painful coming of age by living in a fantasy world. Frankie is left by her father to the care of Berenice, a black woman who serves as her surrogate mother and friend. On Broadway, and in the film, Waters was given top billing. Her portrayal of a Southern mammy-figure could have lapsed into racial stereotype, but in Waters's capable hands the character remained the complex, multifaceted human being created by McCullers.

Maybe Elisabeth did not want to compete with Waters, whom she admired. Perhaps she did not have any serious ambition to become a dramatic actress, but if she had been interested in taking her career in a new direction, *Member* was not going to be the vehicle. At the reading for Richardson, Elisabeth was appalled by the young director's behaviour: "He was mad! He didn't know what he was doing. I couldn't work with him." With Elisabeth out of the running, who else could play the role? She was virtually the only experienced black actress in the country. In the end, Richardson took the daring step of casting a young African American singer called Bertice Reading, who had recently arrived in Britain and scored a success in the West End revue *The Jazz Train* (1955). *Member* opened at the Royal Court Theatre on February 5, 1957. The following year Richardson helped launch the British jazz singer Cleo Laine into "serious" theatre when he cast her in *Flesh to a Tiger*, also at the Royal Court, written by the Jamaican dramatist Barry Reckord.

In 1959 Elisabeth played her first leading role in a West End musical in *The Crooked Mile*. She was cast as the romantic fantasist Sweet Ginger, the owner of an ironmonger's shop. Set in London's Soho, it was a tale of gang warfare in the underworld, and one of the boldest attempts to that date to compete with the Broadway musical. The outstanding music was composed by Peter Greenwell. Peter Wildeblood, who wrote the book (based on his novel *West End People*) and amusing lyrics, drew from his experience of running a club in Soho. Apart from Sweet Ginger, Wildeblood's Damon Runyon-esque characters included Jug Ears (Jack MacGowran), a spineless gang leader loved by Sweet Ginger, and Cora (Millicent Martin), a tart with a heart of gold. Martin, straight from her West End success in *Expresso Bongo*, stole the show.

After a provincial tour that commenced at the Opera House in Manchester on August 11, 1959, *The Crooked Mile* opened at the Cambridge Theatre on September 10. Said Elisabeth: "*The Crooked Mile* was a very happy experience for me. I played opposite Jack MacGowran who was a dear man. It was also the first time that I worked with Millicent Martin and our duet, 'Meet the Family,' got a lot of radio plugs." Says Michael Alexander: "It was directed by Jean Meyer of the Comédie Française, known for his classical work. Lis was able to communicate with him in French. 'Meet the Family,' Lis's duet with Millie Martin, was the big show stopper. In fact it stopped the show cold every night. Lis impressed me with the way she sang the ballad 'If I Ever Fall in Love Again.' She sang it beautifully, and with a full voice. Maybe the show ended because it had a drab setting."

After 164 performances, *The Crooked Mile* closed prematurely on January 30, 1960, in spite of enthusiastic reviews. A cast recording was made on August 16, 1959 (it was the first British cast recording to go on sale on its West End opening night), but in spite of its brilliance, *The Crooked Mile* remained in obscurity for nearly half a century. In 2003 Adrian Wright reissued the 1959 recording on CD on his Must Close Saturday Records label. In his sleeve notes he said:

> *The Crooked Mile* meant business, and—if its first night was anything to go by—it worked. Even the Overture received an ovation. It promised something distinct, brave, pouring out with feeling. It sounded serious. It seemed like real music, with dramatic content and melodies that demanded to be heard. It also had fabulous orchestrations by Gordon Langford which took the score into a class of its own. Never mind that only one of its songs went on to any sort of separate popularity—a terrific duet for the leading ladies, "Meet the Family." There isn't a false note in *The Crooked Mile*, and musically this is one of the strongest and most mature British musicals of the twentieth century.

To promote the CD, on April 28, 2004, *The Crooked Mile* was reassessed by the presenter Edward Seckerson in an edition of his popular BBC Radio 3 series *Stage and Screen*. In the programme, Seckerson, who described the show as a "musical masterpiece," interviewed Peter Greenwell, who recalled:

> I met Peter Wildeblood in 1958. A mutual friend who knew I was looking for a collaborator bumped into him at Covent Garden Opera House, and asked him if he'd ever thought of writing a musical. Peter hadn't, but agreed to meet and discuss. His first words on meeting were, "What are your favourite musicals?" I said *"West Side Story, My Fair Lady,* and *Guys and Dolls."* "Mine too. Done." We hit it off immediately. He was the gentlest, kindest creature imaginable and he never mentioned he had been imprisoned for being homosexual [1954–1955]. I can't imagine what it must have done to him. I had met Elisabeth on previous occasions and I went to her home one afternoon to play her the score and to see if she would agree to appear in it. When I played the score through to her she listened to it very quietly. She didn't say anything and then afterwards she said, "There are a lot of Chinese harmonies, dear. You will make sure I get a clear lead in. Your mother is not very good on Chinese harmonies." So I did make sure she got a cleaner lead in. In the interval on the opening in Manchester, Peter and I overheard someone say "Isn't it marvellous?" Back

came the reply, "Do you think so? Sounds like that *West Side Story* rubbish to me." We were so horrified, and then we said "No. That's the biggest compliment we could ever have!"

After *Dead of Night* (1945), offers to appear in films were practically non-existent, so in 1960 Elisabeth was delighted to be cast in a supporting role as, she recalled, "one of Cleopatra's handmaidens" (possibly Charmian or Iras, she couldn't remember) in *Cleopatra*. A number of entries in Elisabeth's 1960 diary confirm this. For example, on August 22 she was interviewed by the film's director, Rouben Mamoulian, and producer Walter Wanger, at 20th Century Fox's office in London's Soho Square. On August 31 she dined at the home of her friend, the designer Oliver Messel. He had worked on *Glamorous Night*, and in Elisabeth's diary he is credited as the costume designer on *Cleopatra*. Other dinner guests that evening included Mamoulian, Wanger and his wife, the Hollywood film star Joan Bennett, and film director George Cukor. From September 19 to November 25, Elisabeth records at least twelve trips to Pinewood Studios, where the film was being shot. On one occasion (November 7) she notes that Prince Philip and Lord Mountbatten visited the set. On November 25 she enters the following in her diary: "Month's suspension!" Elisabeth later explained that the production had been doomed from the start. Elizabeth Taylor, signed for the title role, insisted on a European base, for tax reasons. Co-starring Peter Finch as Caesar and Stephen Boyd as Mark Antony, the film commenced shooting under the direction of Mamoulian at Pinewood on September 28, 1960. It was officially suspended fifty-two days later. Mamoulian, who had spent a year preparing *Cleopatra*, was said to have been physically sick with apprehension when he saw the set for the Egyptian city of Alexandria in the English countryside, on the outside lot of Pinewood. He resigned on January 18, 1961. Said Elisabeth:

Miss Taylor *never* showed up, and so Mr. Mamoulian had to shoot around her. We were filming in the middle of some bitterly cold English weather, and it was supposed to be Egypt! The skies stayed grey. The sets were soaked in rain. It was a ridiculous situation. I remember the day they brought some beautiful peacocks onto the set, but it was so cold, their feathers started falling off! When a man tried sticking them back on, we couldn't help laughing, even though we felt sorry for the peacocks. Most of the time we [the actors] played cards and waited for Miss Taylor to show up. When it became clear she wasn't going to turn up, they fired Mr. Mamoulian and closed down the production. Later, when they restarted in sunny Italy, Miss Taylor returned to the fold, and they had a new director, Joseph L. Mankiewicz, two new actors, Rex Harrison and Richard Burton, and a new actress for my part! Apparently, before he left,

Mankiewicz asked Mamoulian for advice. "Do as I did," Mamoulian replied. "Resign."

When some of the great American entertainers and musicians visited London, Elisabeth could usually be found in the audience. Diary entries confirm that she saw the following: Judy Garland (Dominion, October 28, 1957); Sammy Davis, Jr. (Pigalle, May 16, 1960); Eartha Kitt (Talk of the Town, October 10, 1960); Ethel Merman (Talk of the Town, February 19, 1964); Pearl Bailey (Talk of the Town, September 20, 1972); the Oscar Peterson Trio (Ronnie Scott's, November 15, 1978); and Peterson again, with Count Basie and Ella Fitzgerald (Royal Festival Hall, September 18, 1982).

Lena Horne was a particular favourite. Elisabeth saw her when she performed at the Hippodrome (April 11, 1961), London Palladium with Tony Bennett (April 30, 1976), and Grosvenor House with Count Basie (July 21, 1979). When Lena brought her award-winning one-woman show *The Lady and Her Music* from Broadway to London, Elisabeth not only attended a performance on August 6, 1984, but met Lena afterwards in her dressing-room. The two legends were fans of each other; in 1989, when Elisabeth celebrated her "eightieth" birthday, Lena sent her a birthday card from New York.

Elisabeth also admired Josephine Baker. On July 28, 1961, while on vacation, she saw Baker at a Sporting Club Gala in Monte Carlo and noted in her diary that Baker sang "Sonny Boy" (once popularised by Al Jolson) and "Dinah." Elisabeth went to see Baker at the London Palladium on August 21, 1974, less than a year before Baker passed away in Paris.

Elisabeth was a keen opera fan and had befriended Leontyne Price in 1952, when that popular diva performed in the first London production of George Gershwin's *Porgy and Bess*. Among the numerous visits to the opera noted in her diary is a performance by Price of *Aida* at Covent Garden on January 10, 1961. In 1987, to mark the tenth anniversary of the death of Maria Callas, Elisabeth and her friend, the opera singer Dame Eva Turner, attended the unveiling of a bust of Callas at the Royal Festival Hall. There were a number of reunions in London with Bricktop, her old friend from Paris, and in 1977 she was reunited with Mabel Mercer, who had accepted a cabaret engagement in London at the Playboy Club.

On May 11, 1962, Elisabeth returned to the famous EMI (formerly HMV) recording studios in London's Abbey Road to participate in a World Record Club recording of *Carmen Jones*. Elisabeth did not sing the operatic role of Carmen Jones. Opera was out of her range. The African American Grace Bumbry sang the role, and Elisabeth, as Carmen's pal Frankie, belted out "Beat Out That Rhythm on a Drum," the song made famous by Pearl Bailey in the 1954 film version. However, the rest of the cast were British-based singers of African Caribbean origin: Thomas Baptiste (Husky Miller), George Webb (Joe), and Ena Babb (Cindy Lou).

Elisabeth's next stage musical, *Cindy-Ella* (or *I Gotta Shoe*), which opened at the Garrick Theatre on December 17, 1962, marked a departure for the singer. It was her first appearance in a stage show with an all-black cast since her London debut in *Dark Doings* in 1933. This jazzed-up version of Cinderella, by Caryl Brahms and Ned Sherrin, co-starred the London-born singer and actress Cleo Laine, Guyanese folk singer and actor Cy Grant, and Trinidadian calypsonian George Browne. An enthusiastic review in the *Spectator* (December 28, 1962) summed up its appeal: "*Cindy's* progress is punctuated by a glowing crop of jazz songs and negro spirituals which the mercurial Miss Laine and her companions put over with dazzling artistry. The effect is of a sophisticated charade." Laine had already established herself as one of Britain's top jazz singers before spreading her wings and branching into straight acting and musical theatre. She had first worked with Elisabeth in a radio play (*Under the Sun*, 1958), and they became great friends. The impact Elisabeth had on other singers is perhaps best summed up by Laine, who as a child in the 1930s had first heard her singing on BBC radio. Interviewed by the author in 1994, she said, "I've always admired Elisabeth. Before I came into the business I used to imitate the way she sang. I loved her voice. When I had the opportunity to work with her, that was a dream come true. She's great fun to be with. Elisabeth has been a mentor to a lot of singers. People in the business adore her." Sherrin had also worked with Elisabeth on radio and television, including the first production of *Cindy-Ella* for BBC radio. Also interviewed by the author in 1994, he recalled:

Caryl and I did it first for radio in 1957, and wrote it for an enormous cast. The lovely Trinidadian singer Lucille Mapp played Cinderella and Elisabeth played the Fairy Godmother. Cy Grant was Prince Charming and Bertice Reading was the narrator. Then Caryl and I adapted it as a novel, and then we did a little excerpt on television in the BBC's *Tonight* programme. We did the whole story in three or four minutes with Elisabeth and Cleo Laine telling the story and singing little snippets of songs. The producer, Michael Codron, saw it and was absolutely fascinated. He rang me up and said, "Couldn't you do that for the two of them in the theatre?" We said, "Well, we don't think we could do it justice with Lis and Cleo, but we could probably do it for four: two men and two women." So George Browne and Cy Grant were added to the cast and we had to put it on very quickly. We decided to stage it as a rehearsed reading but once we started we realised that wouldn't work, so the cast had to learn it. Lis never forgets anything once she's learned it, but banging it into her head is always the hardest thing so Cleo had to stay at Capener's Close and hear Lis's lines until the early hours of the morning. We opened in that awful Winter of 1962–1963 and the snow was high outside the Garrick Theatre. It was a potent combination with Lis, Cleo, Cy, and dear George, who had that wonderful deep voice. It was a very attractive production.

Eleven years separated Elisabeth's brief appearances in the films *Our Man in Havana* (1960) and *Girl Stroke Boy* (1971), but if movie producers ignored her talents, those working in television made brilliant use of them. In fact, television offered Elisabeth some of her richest opportunities in the 1960s.

In 1964 the writer Robert Gould decided to create an original television musical for Elisabeth. In *The Rise and Fall of Nellie Brown*, a young Jamaican girl (Selina) journeys from her loveless home in Liverpool to search for two things: one of them Lillabelle Astor, her famous relative, the "Broadway star who took London by storm," the other the Christmas depicted on an old-fashioned card she has kept for years. Reminiscent of *The Wizard of Oz*, Selina has a Toto-like dog in tow, and on the way she befriends a magician, Jasper Waxo (Ron Moody) and a truck driver (Bryan Mosley). In London, the companions discover that Lillabelle is bedridden and protected by her maid, Nellie Brown, played by Elisabeth. The story ends happily when Nellie reveals that *she* is Lillabelle, masquerading as the star's maid. Interviewed by the author in 1991, Gould explained the background to the play:

In 1950 I started writing special material for Elisabeth's cabaret act, and I always respected her because she always paid me on time. In 1964 I was working at the BBC with the director John Jacobs on his last production there called *The Improbable Mr. Clayville*. He said, "I'm off to work for Anglia television and I want you to write something for me with music for Christmas." I had always wanted to write a musical for Elisabeth and originally wrote *The Rise and Fall of Nellie Brown* as a short novel so that John could decide how to put it together for television. My first choice for the role of Selina was Shirley Bassey. I had met Shirley in 1963 when I shared a taxi with her and Peter Finch returning from the Old Vic production of *Othello* starring the Trinidadian actor Errol John. *Nellie Brown* was really conceived for Elisabeth but then I thought about casting her opposite Shirley who had never acted, but could have been a great actress. However, John's brother, David Jacobs, the BBC disc jockey and presenter of *Juke Box Jury*, had discovered a young, seventeen-year-old Jamaican girl called Millie. She was just a teenager, but she was riding high in the pop charts with her record "My Boy Lollipop." David recommended her to John for the role of Selina, but Millie hadn't acted before. Millie posed a problem because of her lack of experience and training, her strong Jamaican accent, and the fact that she took everything very seriously. Everything was real to her,

not fiction, and she would burst into tears if certain characters in the play upset her. I must say that Elisabeth and Ron Moody were fantastic with her, and
did everything they could to make her feel at ease. They were thoroughly professional, generous to a fault, and it showed in their performances. To their
credit they did not overshadow Millie at all, and everything worked out well.
It is a lovely production and I am very proud of it. Some years later John Guest
at Longman decided he wanted to publish *Nellie Brown* as a full-length children's novel and I gave it a new title, *A Touch of Practical Magic*. It was published in 1973, and I dedicated the book to Elisabeth.

Light-hearted, captivating, and with some catchy songs, *Nellie Brown*
proved to be a Christmas treat for television viewers when it was shown in
ITV's *Play of the Week* series on December 28. However, its 9:10 PM slot prevented it from reaching a young audience, most of whom would have been
in bed. Elisabeth gave a wonderful performance as Nellie/Lillabelle, and the
recording that has survived is a testament to her artistry and star quality.
Other television highlights of the decade included three BBC music programmes in 1966 with Ned Sherrin. *Take a Sapphire* (January 4) was an original musical about the royal Braganzas of nineteenth-century Portugal for
which Sherrin and Caryl Brahms wrote the lyrics, and Ron Grainer provided
the music. Georgia Brown and Max Adrian co-starred. Julian Holland in the
Daily Mail (January 5) commented: "Here at last was the genuine television
musical, something not for ever borrowing and scrimping from the theatre or
the cinema, but something with words and music and song-dancing in its
own right as a piece of television." In her diary entry for the date of the transmission, Elisabeth noted that she watched the programme at Ned's home,
and others in attendance included Caryl Brahms, David Frost, Warren
Beatty, Leslie Caron, Victor Spinetti, and the choreographer Irving Davies,
who had staged the musical numbers for *Take a Sapphire*. Elisabeth was reunited with her *Crooked Mile* co-star Millicent Martin in *The Long Cocktail
Party* (April 23), a glorious revue-style survey of the 1930s as seen through
the eyes of Sherrin and Brahms. John Wood spoke the commentary, David
Kernan co-starred, and the music was arranged and conducted by Peter
Greenwell. An unidentified reviewer in the *Television Mail* (April 29) commented: "Quite who, among these many cooks, was responsible for the curi-
ously plangent musical effect I do not know, but it gave this hour-long recall
of the shows of yesteryear a disturbing and haunting quality. Part of the effect was certainly created by Millicent Martin, attractively different in a
thirty-ish hair style and a Ginger Rogers dress, and by Elisabeth Welch,
whose emotional force seems to grow greater with the passing of time." Towards the end of the year, Elisabeth was reunited with Cleo Laine, Cy Grant,

and George Browne for a television version of their stage hit *Cindy-Ella*, retitled *I Gotta Shoe or Cindy Ella* (December 28). Kenneth Eastaugh in the *Daily Mirror* (December 28) described Elisabeth as "that glistening, solid talent who gave a performance that spelled out in crackling neon letters the word 'professionalism.'" Of the three shows, only *The Long Cocktail Party* has survived in the BBC's archive.

In 1970, when the Hampstead Theatre Club in London presented Noël Coward's *Tonight at Eight*, starring Millicent Martin and Gary Bond, it was suggested that Elisabeth make an appearance in a one-woman show after the performances. Taking the title, *A Marvellous Party*, from one of Coward's songs, the show, devised and directed by Paul Ciani, became a musical history of the 1930s. It incorporated some of Coward's songs and some associated with Elisabeth. Opening on December 30, it marked a turning point in Elisabeth's career, for it became the blueprint for her future one-woman shows. Reviews were excellent. Said B. A. Young in *The Financial Times* (January 4, 1971):

> Any party with Elisabeth Welch as hostess is bound to be marvellous, and this late show at Hampstead certainly is. . . . Miss Welch leans heavily on Cole Porter and Noël Coward for her repertoire and she does them proud. . . . She puts over the lyrics with a sympathy and understanding never heard in the popular singers nowadays. Note especially such details as the *diminuendo* at "every love but true love" in Cole Porter's "Love for Sale," injecting at that climactic point the fundamental tragedy lurking behind the defiant words. This is artistry of a high order.

In February–March 1972 Elisabeth made a rare visit to New York. It was an eventful vacation that included reunions with her pals Alberta Hunter, Bobby Short, and Mabel Mercer, and, on February 27, a birthday party given by her brother John. Guests included her brother Eddie and his wife Miriam. During the trip, Elisabeth attended performances of the following Broadway productions: *Follies* (February 24), *Viva Viva Regina* (March 1), and *No No Nanette* (March 2), as well as a Carnegie Hall concert by her friend and Kinnerton Street neighbour Leontyne Price (March 5).

On October 30, 1973, at Her Majesty's Theatre, Elisabeth made a long-overdue return to West End musicals as Berthe in *Pippin*, with music and lyrics by Stephen Schwartz, the composer of *Godspell*. The Broadway version had opened on October 23, 1972, and won several Tony awards. It ran for 1,944 performances; it was still running when the London version went into production. On Broadway, Berthe had been played by Irene Ryan, who stopped the show with the rousing, vaudeville sing-along "No Time at All."

True to form, in London, Elisabeth stopped the show cold with her rendition. Cicely Courtneidge had originally been cast as Berthe, but her agent asked for too much money, so Ned Sherrin put Elisabeth's name forward. At first she was horrified. In the late 1960s and early 1970s she suffered very badly from arthritis in the hips: "I told Ned I couldn't do it. I cannot go limping onto a stage. I was embarrassed but Ned practically pushed me in there to audition and I had never auditioned before."

After fifty years in show business, Elisabeth's first audition (described as a "rehearsal" in her diary) took place on May 17, 1973, at Her Majesty's Theatre in the presence of Bob Fosse. He had just won the Tony award (on March 25) for directing the Broadway version of *Pippin*, quickly followed by a Best Director Oscar (on March 27) for the film *Cabaret*. Elisabeth, accompanied by Peter Greenwell on the piano, sang "Solomon" from *Nymph Errant* and "If I Ever Fall in Love Again" from *The Crooked Mile*. Afterwards she took great pleasure in telling everyone what had happened: "After singing 'Solomon' I made a terrible *faux pas*. When Bob Fosse asked 'What was that song?' I replied 'Oh, you're too young to know, it's a little song Cole Porter wrote for me.'" Each time Elisabeth described this encounter, she burst into fits of laughter. According to Greenwell, Fosse responded to Elisabeth's *faux pas* with, "I do beg your pardon. I'm so sorry." He came up onto the stage to inform her, "I'd love you to play this part in the show."

Says Michael Alexander: "I went to see *Pippin* on the second night but I was told that on the opening night Lis received a huge ovation after singing 'No Time at All,' causing a long delay. Bob Fosse was livid. Lis said he was very strict after that. There'd be no encores. It was disappointing because it was her only song in the show. The big trouble with *Pippin* was that Northern J. Calloway was so dreary. He had no charm like Ben Vereen in the Broadway version." Reviews were mixed, but critics were unanimous in their praise of Elisabeth. "Elisabeth Welch produces the goods and stops the show with a style and panache too rarely seen on stage these days," said Jack Tinker in the *Daily Mail* (October 31). An unidentified reviewer in the *Sunday Times* (November 4) summarised: "*Pippin* is a mini-pantomime, childish before the interval, and simple-minded afterwards. It was a mistake on the first night to exasperate the audience by not allowing Elisabeth Welch to have an encore." Said Elisabeth:

> Unfortunately *Pippin* did not go as well as we had hoped. It had fabulous orchestrations, and a terrific cast, including Paul Jones, Patricia Hodge, and Diane Langton, but London did not like it. We lasted just over three months. I was suffering with arthritis and using a stick when I went into *Pippin*, but the

stage hands at Her Majesty's were adorable. They guided me to my place and sometimes one of them would carry me across but I must say once I left my walking stick in the wing, it's extraordinary how people in our business overcome such things. I've seen very ill people practically carried to an entrance in the theatre and once they get on stage they forget they're ill and that's how it was with me. I forgot about the arthritis and sang my song. This is the greatness of the theatre, it clears your brain and takes all the pains away and I was very much in pain. In 1974 I went and had two hip operations. When the surgeon saw the X-rays he couldn't believe it, the bones were so rotten. I'm a quick healer, thank God. He said wait another nine months and you'll feel a new woman, and he was dead right.

Elisabeth continued working steadily throughout the rest of the decade. She recorded her first long-playing album, *Elisabeth Welch*, for World Records in December 1975. This long-overdue compilation included her first recordings of "Love for Sale," "*La Vie en Rose*," "Twentieth Century Blues," and "No Time at All." A follow-up, *Soft Lights and Sweet Music*, was recorded in June 1976.

On stage she joined Linda Lewis and Clarke Peters for a revival of *Cindy-Ella* (1976) at the Criterion, and she played Fatimah, the wise woman, in Sandy Wilson's musical *Aladdin* (1979) at the Lyric, Hammersmith. For BBC radio she played the magical Mrs. Yajnavalkya, an exotic masseuse, in Sandy Wilson's musical *Valmouth* (1975); narrated the series *Portrait of Piaf* (1976); and was the subject of an edition of the series *The Leading Ladies* (1977). On television she joined Ned Sherrin and David Kernan for *Song by Song by Lorenz Hart* (1978) and was interviewed in a BBC documentary, *Paul Robeson* (1978).

It may seem hard to believe, but Elisabeth had to wait until November 26, 1979, before she made her first appearance in a Royal Variety Performance. Though she had been one of Britain's brightest stage stars for five decades and a personal favourite of the Queen Mother, she had been constantly overlooked when the star-studded galas were presented to members of the Royal Family. The 1979 edition was staged—for the first time—at the Theatre Royal, Drury Lane, in the presence of Queen Elizabeth II; it was televised on December 2. Elisabeth performed Noël Coward's "Twentieth Century Blues," and others taking part that year included Yul Brynner and Virginia McKenna with members of *The King and I* company, Carol Channing, Elaine Stritch, Ned Sherrin, David Kernan, Millicent Martin, and Julia McKenzie.

At the end of the decade—just before she made an impact in Derek Jarman's *The Tempest* (see chapter 9)—Elisabeth made two brief film appearances. In *Revenge of the Pink Panther* (1978), directed by Blake Edwards, she shared a scene with Peter Sellers (as Inspector Clouseau) as Mrs. Wu, a Chinese madame who runs a whore house. In *Arabian Adventure* (1979) she was unrecognisable in heavy make-up as the Beggarwoman. Eric Braun recognised her name in the cast list and welcomed her appearance in his review in *Films and Filming* (July 1979):

> "I'm hungry—spare some food for a poor old woman." The voice is unmistakable. But who could be behind the ragged bundle of clothes, the warty visage and bent posture of this gnarled Beggarwoman? It couldn't possibly be . . . but, come the credit titles, and it is—none other than Elisabeth Welch, famous in revue since New York's *Blackbirds*, and very under-used in films since co-starring with Paul Robeson over here in the thirties. The little orphan boy Majeed (Puneet Sira) reluctantly hands her the peach he has just acquired, and she disappears as the fruit falls to the ground and turns into a magic sapphire, within which she has been transformed into the beautiful Jinnee Vahishta. Only she isn't Elisabeth Welch any longer, but Capucine—thereby effecting one of the strangest transmutations in screen history. It's always nice to welcome one of Capucine's now very rare film appearances, even as here seen briefly through a sapphire, tiny, angular and blue-rinsed, but why couldn't Ms Welch effect her own metamorphosis, as she's not only still one of the most melodious singers in the business, but comely with it and well able to do her own fairy-godmothering, one would think.

~

CHAPTER NINE

Derek Jarman and *The Tempest*

The Goddess of High Camp

Nothing could be more camp than the sight of Elisabeth as the "Goddess" in Derek Jarman's low-budget, unorthodox film of William Shakespeare's *The Tempest*. Dressed in gold from head to foot and surrounded by handsome young sailors, the Goddess interrupts Miranda and Ferdinand's wedding feast, walks through a rain of confetti in a room garlanded with flowers, and sings "Stormy Weather." Writer and jazz singer George Melly described this sequence in *The Independent* magazine (May 13, 1989) as "arguably the campest, most sparkling moment in the history of cinema." Jarman told the *Evening Standard* (April 24, 1980): "She's a real love goddess. She's high art, not kitsch. You're supposed to laugh at that scene and express disbelief. Life isn't deadly serious, you know."

Jarman first heard Elisabeth sing "Stormy Weather" on December 17, 1978, in a concert at the Royal Opera House in Covent Garden, a benefit for the Friends of Covent Garden Opera. Afterwards, at a party at Frederick Ashton's home, Jarman heard her sing Ruth Etting's famous torch song "Ten Cents a Dance." Ashton told the young director all about her, and Jarman invited her to appear in his film:

> Derek rang me up and asked me if I wanted to sing in *The Tempest*. I said, "What tempest?" He said, "Shakespeare's *Tempest*." I said, "You must be mad! What do you want me to sing?" He said, "'Stormy Weather.'" I said, "You're joking," but I went ahead with it and we had a lot of fun. I knew his name, and

that he was a great art person who had made a couple of films. I was aware that he was successful, but unusual and unconventional. Derek was a good director and anyone with any sense wants that. We had rapport immediately.

Jarman's *Tempest* was the first attempt to film Shakespeare's last play. To keep within his minuscule budget (£150,000), the director freely adapted—and simplified—the text and cut it to run for only an hour and a half. The result is an exquisite, bizarre, atmospheric film of great beauty, tension, and comedy.

Elisabeth arrived on location on February 15, 1979, and completed the "Stormy Weather" sequence in four days, returning home on February 19:

> We filmed it in Stoneleigh Abbey near Kenilworth in Warwickshire, a beautiful house and an inspired choice for Prospero's magic castle! We had three feet of snow and we stayed at a hotel in Coventry but the boys who played the sailors got lost on the way to the location. They were only hired for the day and by the time they arrived it was too late to film anything. Derek couldn't afford to put them in our hotel, so they had to buy sleeping bags and toothbrushes when they found they had to stay overnight. They slept in the Abbey. It must have been freezing! I adored my sailor boys. Some of them were in their early twenties, some of them in their teens. They gave me such a warm feeling. On the set they were sweet and made me feel good. They treated me as a Queen! I had a good rapport with them and this made the filming easy and lots of fun. Derek was easy to work with too, and he loved his work. He directed in his shirt sleeves with his braces on and I loved him. He was a gentle, highly intelligent man. Boyish. Not aggressive like some film personalities. In his public life he could give a hard time to those he disliked, and enjoy it, too, and so did we because we didn't like who he didn't like. Derek drew me to him and I believed in him, and trusted him. If he'd told me to stand on my head I would have! I wanted to hug him, and I did occasionally.

The feeling was mutual. In 1984 Jarman paid tribute to Elisabeth in his journal *Dancing Ledge*, quoting from his 1979 diary:

> She entranced all the young sailor boys at the marriage party—her singing was an enchantment. Yolanda's bright-orange dress illuminated her like a fiery moon. In the cold ballroom she worked non-stop through the day, never missing a cue; and still had the energy to entertain everyone at the dinner-table in the refectory. "One song Welch," as she called herself, had one song in *The Tempest* and true to form she stopped the show.

In her diary entry for February 18, 1979, Elisabeth wrote: "7.30 AM—car—Stoneleigh Abbey. 6.00 PM *Tempest*—Ballroom *finis!*"

On May 1, 1980, following film festival screenings in Edinburgh, Toronto, and London in 1979, and Berlin in February 1980, *The Tempest* was commercially released in London, at The Screen on the Hill in Hampstead. In the press release Jarman gave some insights into his creation of this unusual but compelling film:

I have always felt that Shakespeare translates rather badly into film. There is a great rift between the artificiality of stage conventions and the naturalism of film settings. Of all the Shakespeare films, *Henry V*, which recognised this problem, is my favourite. In Stoneleigh Abbey we found what I feel could be the most perfect metaphor for the island, and in the dunes of Bamborough, a landscape that was universal and abstract. Both settings allowed the verse to breathe, and neither conflicted with it in detail. . . . None of the actors attempted to give conventional theatrical performances. . . . This was reinforced by living and working in Stoneleigh Abbey for four weeks in February. . . . I think the Abbey left strong and happy memories with us all. Creeping through the dilapidated candle-lit rooms at night; watching Yolanda Sonnabend creating Toyah's beautiful costume miraculously out of a few fragments; the hibernating butterflies awakened by [director of photography] Peter Middleton's lamps; the candle-lit ballroom suddenly alive and glittering as Elisabeth Welch enabled us to remember that *The Tempest*, whatever it might have become, was once the perfect entertainment for a cold December night.

There were some detractors. Felix Barker wrote in the *Evening News* (May 1, 1980): "I rather wish the director hadn't imported a chorus of white uniformed modern sailors among whom Elisabeth Welch, a dusky vision in gold, wandered singing 'Stormy Weather.' This touch of the Ken Russells is just the sort of stunt that a good artist must resist." Jarman responded to his critics with the following statement: "I didn't set out to be loved—just to get a reaction!" Fortunately, intelligent critics appreciated the film, including David Robinson. He described *The Tempest* in *The Times* (May 2, 1980) as "the most truly spectacular British film for years. Spectacle, you discover in Jarman's work, is a product of the artistic imagination, not of millions of dollars' worth of scenery and plaster. . . . *The Tempest* stands alongside the *Hamlet* and *Lear* of the Soviet director Grigori Kozintsev as one of the most successful, authentic and truly poetic adaptations of Shakespeare. . . . My enthusiasm for this rare film is unrepentant and unqualified, not least because it arrives in a British cinema that has rarely much to boast about."

Regrettably, the film was not a success in the United States. It suffered from a scathing review from Vincent Canby, film critic for the *New York Times*

(September 22, 1980), after it was screened in the New York Film Festival. He stated that the film "would be funny if it weren't unbearable. It's a fingernail scratched along a blackboard. . . . There are [sic] no poetry, no ideas, no characterisations, no narrative, no fun." Canby's vicious attack on the film killed it in the United States and made it impossible for Jarman to raise money for his next feature film project.

On a happier note, the publicity surrounding the film gave Elisabeth a new lease on life and a whole new legion of fans, but for Jarman the indifference and unsupportiveness of the film industry meant that it would be seven years before he directed another feature film. *Caravaggio* (1986) was released in the same year Jarman was diagnosed HIV positive. Though he continued making films, AIDS cut short his wonderful, remarkable career on February 19, 1994. He was just fifty-two. A few months later, Elisabeth participated in a television tribute to the director, Channel 4's *A Night with Derek*.

For *The Tempest*, Jarman had wanted to cast Sir John Gielgud as Prospero, but the great Shakespearean actor declined. Jarman's biographer, Tony Peake, reveals that Gielgud would never admit to the fact that he did not really see eye to eye with Jarman or like the script. Gielgud wrote to Jarman to say that he found the script "full of ingenious compressions and imaginative ideas but I'm afraid I couldn't agree to playing it." It would later upset Jarman that Gielgud would agree to play Prospero for his "rival" Peter Greenaway in *Prospero's Books* (1990).

So, in *The Tempest* Elisabeth could have been reunited with Sir John Gielgud, her wartime co-star in *Christmas Party* in Gibraltar, but it was not to be. However, a few years later, on September 1, 1985, Elisabeth and Gielgud found themselves—at the invitation of Vanessa Redgrave—at the Old Vic Theatre in *A Tribute to Sir Michael Redgrave*. In a cast that also included Wendy Hiller, Rachel Kempson, Ian McKellen, and Peggy Ashcroft, Elisabeth sang, and Gielgud closed the programme with a speech by Prospero from *The Tempest*. Backstage, in a tiny dressing-room, Elisabeth finally managed to speak to Gielgud on the subject of her Shakespearean debut: "I said, 'I've got to ask you, John. Did you see me in *The Tempest?*' and he replied, in that stentorian Gielgud voice, 'Oh, Elisabeth, why did you do it?' 'Well, it had Shakespeare's lines,' I responded. 'I suppose so,' he said. Then we fell about laughing." In her diary entry for that evening, Elisabeth confirms that Gielgud gave her a lift home in his chauffeur-driven car.

The final word (or words) about Elisabeth and *The Tempest* should be given to the critics and writers who have praised her unusual but memorable appearance in the film. Here are just a few quotations.

David Robinson (*The Times*, May 2 1980):

Jarman saves his most audacious stroke to the end. When he introduces his Goddess at the nuptials of Ferdinand and Miranda we are naturally expecting some jewelled deity of Jacobean masque. Instead there is Miss Elisabeth Welch . . . singing "Stormy Weather." The inevitable first reaction is a titter of disbelief and embarrassment. But Jarman knows his Goddess. The surprise and embarrassment are instantly banished by the spell and authority of this perennially genial performer. . . . Jarman rightly perceives that, if he wants to give us the sense of a celestial descent, he will do it best through such a transcendent artist and spellbinding presence.

Richard Barkley (*Sunday Express*, May 4, 1980):

[*The Tempest*] fails to capture the imagination until an inconsequential but extraordinarily vivid final sequence which has a bunch of sailors whirling about in a folk dance and Elisabeth Welch giving an exquisite rendering of "Stormy Weather" that on its own is just about worth your money.

David Castell (*Sunday Telegraph*, May 4, 1980):

The Goddesses have been given their cards. All except one and she, I venture to suggest, is the Goddess of High Camp—the indestructible Elisabeth Welch whose honeyed voice can still weave a potent spell as she sings "Stormy Weather" to a chorus of horn-piping matelots—a delicious conceit.

Samuel Crowl (*Shakespeare on Film Newsletter*, December 1980):

I found Caliban at his mother's pap intrusive and unnecessary but thought Miss Welch's "Stormy Weather" inspired. Its refrain "Keeps rainin' all the time" became a wonderful modern equivalent for Feste's corrective to *Twelfth Night's* midsummer madness: "the rain it raineth every day." This moment worked because it created a witty resonance with all those other moments in the comedies where, in the midst of the festive celebration of love and romance, Shakespeare carefully places reminders that holiday is not every day; that men are April when they woo but December when they wed; that maids are May when they are maids but the sky changes when they are wives.

Michael O'Pray (*Derek Jarman: Dreams of England*, BFI, 1996):

The Tempest is one of Jarman's most accomplished and satisfying films. Elisabeth Welch's rendering of "Stormy Weather" is one of the great scenes in British cinema, its majestic quality throwing into relief the other levels of representation within the film from nineteenth-century Romanticism to Hollywood pastiche to high camp.

William Pencak (*The Films of Derek Jarman*, McFarland, 2002):

The pièce de résistance, however, is the singing of "Stormy Weather" by Elisabeth Welch. . . . Sorcery, disguised perhaps as entertainment, is indeed required to keep the Brave New World in line. And sorcery is exactly what Welch performs, with her extraordinarily seductive singing. She sings of stormy weather with a smile on her face. Her manner, although not the words of the song, conforms to the general meaning of Shakespeare's original masque ("Lis replaced Iris, Ceres, and Juno," Jarman noted), which is to serve as a prelude to a calm voyage back to Europe and prosperity and peace all around. Welch seems to be the African, non-European who has been co-opted as a star performer, but she and Jarman give us an opportunity to read beyond presentation of the song to think about the actual words.

CHAPTER TEN

~

Renaissance

If the music and the lyric are lovely, then it's the song for me.

The publicity surrounding Elisabeth's appearance in Derek Jarman's *The Tempest* contributed to a renaissance in her career in Britain. Meanwhile, she enjoyed a brief "comeback" in New York, joining the once-in-a-lifetime cast of *Black Broadway* at the Town Hall (from May 1 to 24, 1980). This was her first professional appearance in New York since 1931. Staged originally at the 1979 Newport Jazz Festival (without Elisabeth), this vaudeville-style revue was a song-and-dance salute not only to the old-style black show music but to some of the artists who had graced Broadway since the turn of the century.

The master of ceremonies was Elisabeth's friend, the popular cabaret entertainer Bobby Short, who also co-produced and co-directed. Tap dancer Honi Coles appeared and choreographed. Among the veterans appearing in the show were the tap-dancing legend John W. Bubbles, of Buck and Bubbles fame, and the singer Edith Wilson. Bubbles had been the original Sportin' Life in *Porgy and Bess* (1935) and took part in *Black Broadway* despite being partially paralysed. Sitting in a chair he reprised "It Ain't Necessarily So." Known as the "Father of Soul Tap," Bubbles died in 1986 at the age of eighty-four. Wilson had made her debut on the Town Hall stage in 1921 in *Put and Take*. She later starred on Broadway in *Hot Chocolates* (1929) with Louis Armstrong and Fats Waller. She died in 1981 at the age of eighty-five. In addition to Elisabeth and Adelaide Hall, who both travelled from London to take part, a younger generation of talent lent able support to the veterans: dancer Gregory Hines and Nell Carter, who had been nominated for a Tony in 1978 for *Ain't Misbehavin'*, a celebration of the music of Fats Waller. Michael Alexander journeyed to New York to see the show:

> Lis appeared twice in *Black Broadway*. In the first half, dressed in red, Gregory Hines gave her a nice introduction and she sang "Love for Sale" and "Solomon." Then she sang "Charleston" which she had introduced in *Runnin' Wild* in 1923, but Lis explained to the audience that she thought the lyrics were awful! The most beautiful thing happened in the second half. Lis led Edith Wilson onto the stage and sang, beautifully, "Silver Rose," the song that Florence Mills popularised. In 1926 Edith sang as a back up to Florence when she introduced this song in *Blackbirds*, and Edith did the same for Lis. It caused a big storm. The applause was deafening. Lis looked so lovely. *Black Broadway* did her a lot of good in America. Everyone was very impressed with her charm and artistry. That is, everyone except Nell Carter, who was also in the cast. She was vulgar and jealous of Lis, and backstage treated her with contempt.

In London in 1982 Elisabeth made a triumphant appearance in her one-woman show at the Riverside Studios in Hammersmith. However, the turning point in her "renaissance" was her appearance in the critically acclaimed revue *Jerome Goes to Hollywood* at the Donmar Warehouse Theatre in London's Covent Garden in 1985. It was the brainchild of David Kernan, the actor, singer, and producer, who had been described as "Britain's foremost interpreter of Stephen Sondheim." In 1975 Kernan had played Carl-Magnus in the London production of *A Little Night Music*; following a successful London run, he made his Broadway debut in *Side by Side by Sondheim* (1977). His production company, Show People, introduced the Broadway legend Barbara Cook to London audiences and presented Ian McKellen's hugely successful solo show *Acting Shakespeare*. Conceived by Kernan as a centenary tribute to Jerome Kern, *Jerome Goes to Hollywood* opened on May 28, 1985. Kernan told *Plays and Players* (July 1985):

> The format is very much like *Side by Side by Sondheim*—a small scale and intimately staged musical, involving three or four people, singing songs and giving anecdotes about the composers, about the shows. It could be general, it could be a specific period. *Jerome Goes to Hollywood* just takes that time in the composer's life and uses songs he composed for the movies. . . . We want to keep these shows small—when we took *Side by Side* to New York, for example, they wanted to expand it, and I said "no, we must maintain the intimacy of it" and

we did. I think there's a huge market for small scale musical entertainments, and heaven knows lots of good people to do them—I called around and asked some mates to be in *Jerome* and ended up with Elaine Delmar, Liz Robertson and Elisabeth Welch, which was heaven.

Kernan had already worked with Elisabeth on television before he invited her to appear in the revue, and it was the perfect vehicle for her. Dick Vosburgh supplied the witty linking material that spiced the show with just the right amount of anecdote and information, but the emphasis was on the thirty-seven songs, brilliantly delivered by the cast of four. Critics raved, and without exception they singled out Elisabeth. Said Mike Mills in *What's On in London* (June 6–12, 1985): "Elisabeth Welch . . . is a phenomenon. In a world of illusion and fake sentiment, she is the real thing, a singer whose vitality and humour, humanity and dignity shine through everything she does. She sings sweet and true as ever and when she chooses she can make anyone else on stage disappear."

Scheduled for a limited run, such was the success of *Jerome* that it was renamed *Kern Goes to Hollywood* and re-opened at the Donmar on July 22. It proved to be one of the busiest days in Elisabeth's career. According to her diary, Elisabeth attended an afternoon rehearsal at the Donmar before being whisked off to the BBC's Shepherd's Bush Theatre—in her stage make-up and costume—for an early evening appearance in Terry Wogan's popular live talk show, *Wogan*. After performing "Smoke Gets in Your Eyes," Elisabeth was interviewed by Wogan. She was at her most animated and entertaining. After sharing memories of Gertrude Lawrence, she recalled the opening night of *Glamorous Night* and her appearance in Derek Jarman's *The Tempest* before being whisked back to the Donmar for "curtain up" at 7.30 PM. Jack Tinker described the second edition of the revue in the *Daily Mail* (July 24, 1985) as a "joyous musical entertainment." He too raved about Elisabeth: "The sight and sound of Miss Elisabeth Welch discarding her microphone to croon a sweet, unaccompanied version of 'I Told Every Little Star' is a moment of daunting theatre magic. Miss Welch, who in her time has sung the best, by the best and with the best, gives an object lesson on how to achieve the most by apparently doing the least. . . . Watch her tease her audience with 'She Didn't Say Yes' and know all there is to learn about style." For *Kern Goes to Hollywood*, Elisabeth was nominated for a Laurence Olivier Award in the category of Outstanding Performance by an Actress in a Musical (see "Awards and Tributes").

On August 13, 1985, during the run of *Kern Goes to Hollywood* at the Donmar Warehouse, disaster struck. Elisabeth returned home after the show that evening to face one of the most devastating experiences of her life. She was mugged:

> I was bashed, just as I was entering my house. I was about to put my key in the door and I heard this person behind me. I said, "Excuse me, who are you look-ing for?" And he said, "Number 2" and as he spoke he came to me and that's all I remember. When I regained consciousness I was in my neighbour's house. He'd punched me in the face and thank goodness I was unconscious because I'm saved from the memory. There's no memory. He'd taken my handbag con-taining about £12, credit cards, and stage jewellery.

Elisabeth was taken to Westminster Hospital suffering from shock, cuts, and bruises. At first doctors feared she had a fractured skull. Elisabeth coped by "wiping" it from her memory: "I never spoke about it. I was lucky I had the theatre to go to."

In spite of her terrible ordeal, Elisabeth was determined that the show would go on. On August 14 she discharged herself from hospital, and that evening was back on stage at the Donmar Warehouse: "I'm an old soldier. I'm not going to let it put me off. I have a hole in my lip, but I let out a few hollers when I got home and knew I could still sing. I believe we live in a more violent society. There's no respect any more, unfortunately. It worries me when I meet it. Not for me, because I can cope with it. I worry for other people, who do not cope."

In a private letter to Elisabeth dated August 16, 1985, Sir John Gielgud wrote:

> Dear Liz
> I was so very distressed to hear and read of your wretched experience. I do so hope you are none the worse and able to get back to the show, for which you had such splendid reviews. I was enchanted at seeing you in the sailor number of Derek Jarman's *Tempest*, which was the only thing in it that I thoroughly en-joyed. I think often of our days in Gibraltar so long ago and wish I was more often in London so that I could see and hear you again in person. Take care of yourself.
> My love and admiration as ever
> John Gielgud

On October 21, 1985, Elisabeth travelled to Los Angeles to take part in an-other tribute to Jerome Kern, this one called *Jerome Kern: A Centennial Cele-bration*. Presented at the Samuel Goldwyn Theatre by the Academy of Motion Picture Arts and Sciences, the concert included vintage Kern film extracts and live performances. Accompanied by Michael Feinstein on piano, Elisabeth stopped the show with "Smoke Gets in Your Eyes" and "She Didn't Say Yes." When Steven Smith of the *Los Angeles Times* (October 19, 1985) asked her why it had taken so long to make her first trip to Hollywood, she replied, "I let all my Los Angeles friends visit me. They have more money than I do!" She added: "Kern's absolutely beautiful for your vocal cords and he chose some of our best lyric writers to match his beautiful notes." On November 25, 1985, Elisabeth performed "Smoke Gets in Your Eyes" for her second appearance in a Royal Variety Performance. Queen Elizabeth II attended the star-studded gala at the Theatre Royal, Drury Lane, which was televised on December 1.

Meanwhile, Elisabeth received the surprise of her life when she was the subject of one of Britain's most popular television shows, *This Is Your Life*. Recorded on October 8 and televised on November 6, the programme, hosted by Eamon Andrews, included tributes from Elaine Delmar, Liz Robertson, Adelaide Hall, Mary Ellis, Peter Graves, Betty Driver, Hermione Baddeley, Tommy Trinder, June Whitfield, Paul Jones, Cleo Laine, and John Dankworth. Evelyn Laye closed the show with the following tribute: "I've admired you since the Cochran days. I saw everything you ever did. I saw the last thing that you have just done [*Kern Goes to Hollywood*] and you were equally as great. Great you are! But the thing that I've loved more than anything over the years is the charming friendship that we've had together and may it long go on, my dear." Lena Horne, friend and fan, appeared in a pre-recorded tribute. There was a big surprise when John Welch greeted his sister—in person—having travelled from his home in New York. Looking more beautiful and animated than ever, Elisabeth was overwhelmed and in tears throughout:

> It was absolutely fantastic. Wonderful. It was such a surprise. If I'd known it was going to happen I wouldn't have been there! It's terrifying. I didn't know how I'd get down those stairs at the beginning. Eamon Andrews told me to put my hand on his arm because it was a long flight of stairs through the audience to the stage with no banisters. I'd already been crying with nerves in the dressing-room. When I walked onto the stage I was absolutely shivering. It was marvellous afterwards because then I got to talk to everybody. When I came home I sat in a chair and I was in shock for about an hour and a half. Then I went to bed and didn't sleep.

More adulation followed for Elisabeth when the Donmar Warehouse revue, now called *Jerome Kern Goes to Hollywood*, transferred to Broadway. Opening at the Ritz Theatre on January 23, 1986, it was Elisabeth's first appearance in New York since *Black Broadway* in 1980. Sadly, the show—with Scott Holmes replacing Kernan—met with an indifferent reception. Critics didn't feel that it was imaginative or exciting enough for Broadway. It quickly closed, after thirteen performances, on February 1. However, the critics adored Elisabeth, and her performance prompted Frank Rich of the *New York Times* (January 24, 1986) to make his famous comment: "We must write letters to our Congressmen demanding that Miss Welch be detained in the United States forthwith, as a national resource too rare and precious for export." He added that her elegant phrasing suggested "a second coming of Mabel Mercer." In spite of the show's failure, it was a memorable homecoming for Elisabeth, who was nominated for a Tony, Broadway's equivalent of the Oscar (see "Awards and Tributes"). New York didn't want to let her go:

> A lot of nightclub people came after me, but I can't do two performances a night at my age and someone suggested a one-woman show. I think Lucille Lortel actually was the one who planted the bug. She asked would I come and play at her theatre, but I had no music and no clothes, so I went home to London for a week and came back to do the show. Things keep happening to me like that. I don't script anything and that's why I'm all over the stage. I did this show in a tiny theatre in London. My original idea was not to be a diva upon the stage, but somebody who's in a large room with a lot of friends.

Elisabeth's one-woman show, *A Time to Start Living*, ran at the Lucille Lortel Theatre for a limited season, from March 20 to April 13, and earned her several honours (see "Awards and Tributes"), including one from New York's Outer Critics Circle "for making old song favorites young, fresh, and vital." Stephen Holden described her performance in an enthusiastic review in the *New York Times* (March 26, 1986):

> Miss Welch is full of innocent mischief. She performs with a gleam in her eye, a raised eyebrow and a smile full of secrets. . . . While her singing contains elements of the blues, her style is more that of an expatriate bohemian in the parlor tradition of Mabel Mercer. . . . The show is atypical of one-woman retrospectives as exemplified by Lena Horne's Broadway show. Running a little over an hour without an intermission, it is a modest cabaret act brought to the stage with no fancy production values. . . . While Miss Welch's voice isn't large, she has a seamless legato and unfailingly elegant diction. Her singing is graceful and precise and infused always with an air of sly, wistful amusement. . . . Miss Welch's blend of English refinement and eroticism is superbly matched to the dark comic songs of Porter and Rodgers and Hart. . . . But her straight ballad performances . . . are just as impressive and suffused with an optimism that seems to emanate from the core of her being. "I believe if I refuse to grow old, I can be young till I die," Miss Welch sings in the show's title song. The way Miss Welch sings these words, they aren't the cozily sentimental homilies of a sweet little old lady, but a still-vital woman's sly strategy for tricking time.

Elisabeth at the age of three with her brother Edward (1907)

Elisabeth singing "Charleston" in *Runnin' Wild* (1923)

Lew Leslie's *Blackbirds*, Moulin Rouge, Paris (1929)

Elisabeth, Berlin (1932)

Elisabeth, London (1933)

MISS
ELISABETH
WELCH

Arthur Ferrier caricature (1933)

Soft Lights and Sweet Music (1935) (from left to right) Bill Shakespeare, Reginald Leopold, Austen Croom-Johnson, Elisabeth, Eric Siday, and Albert Harris

"The Girl I Knew" from *Glamorous Night* (1935)

Elisabeth (1936)

"Yesterday's Thrill" from *Soft Lights and Sweet Music* (1936)

"Roll Up Sailor Man" from *Big Fella* (1937)

No Time for Comedy, Haymarket Theatre (1941) (from left to right) Cecil Madden, Gerry Wilmot, Rex Harrison, Diana Wynyard, Carol Reed, Elisabeth, and Lilli Palmer

Elisabeth singing to Griffith Jones and Ann Dvorak in *This Was Paris* (1942)

Gibraltar (1942) (from left to right) Elisabeth, Jeanne de Casalis, Phyllis Stanley, unknown, Beatrice Lillie, Michael Wilding, Edith Evans, John Gielgud, unknown

Elisabeth (1944)

Elisabeth (1945)

Elisabeth (1946)

Oranges and Lemons (1949)

Café de Paris, London (1954) (from left to right) Denholm Elliott, Anne Leon, Anthony Forwood, Elisabeth, Dirk Bogarde, and "Ginny"

Elisabeth at home in Cottage Walk, off Sloane Street (1957)

Elisabeth with Jack MacGowran in *The Crooked Mile* (1959)

Elisabeth with Ron Moody in *The Rise and Fall of Nellie Brown* (1964)

Elisabeth in *The Tempest* (1979)

Elisabeth with Derek Jarman (1979)

Elisabeth with Adelaide Hall and Honi Coles in London (1981)

Elisabeth and Queen Elizabeth II, Royal Variety Performance at the Theatre Royal, Drury Lane (1985)

Keeping Love Alive (1987)

Elisabeth receiving a special award from the Variety Club of Great Britain at the London Hilton Hotel (1989)

Elisabeth and George Melly at Denville Hall (1996). *Photo by Robert Taylor*

While Elisabeth was enjoying her triumphant return to New York, her friend Cleo Laine was starring on Broadway as Princess Puffer in the musical *The Mystery of Edwin Drood*. Laine recalled in her autobiography, *Cleo* (1994):

> Elisabeth Welch stayed with me at the time New York feted her and her one-woman show. She was divine company, a laugh a minute, and her memory for dates and lyrics was unchallengeable. As I found out when I swore we [had] opened in *Cindy Ella* at the Arts Theatre and she told me, "You're wrong, gal, it was the Garrick." Still not convinced she was right we had a bet. I asked Tony Walton, the designer, who looked through some old records for me and said, "You have lost the bet I'm afraid, Cleo, she's right." Elisabeth became the belle of New York that season.

Around this time Elisabeth commented on her audiences and influences:

> It amazes me that so many young people come to my concerts. Friends come, and people who have heard of me come but most of the new ones are very young people and that gives me a thrill. That knocks me for six. It's very difficult even to control my emotions when I see these youngsters in the audience, especially when they wait to see me afterwards. I am very moved by it. And a lot of them come backstage to greet me. They like the songs and the stories I tell about the men who wrote them, like Cole Porter, Ivor Novello, Irving Berlin and Jerome Kern. In the old days people stood back. They didn't approach you. I was protected because of the times. Now they want to talk to you, and touch you. Mind you, I like to see my old friends as well. They can also be spontaneous and the New York audiences were fantastic because they didn't know me there at all. People say "we always hear your words." Why shouldn't you hear the words? They're there, they should be heard. If the lyric and the music are lovely, then it's the song for me. I like Cole Porter, Rodgers and Hart, Noël Coward, George Gershwin, Jerome Kern, and Irving Berlin. How can you fail if you've got any of those in your repertoire? My favourite would have to be Cole Porter because he was the nearest to me. I've often wondered what inspired that generation. If I have to name a favourite singer it would have to be Frank Sinatra. I like what he does with a song. It's exactly what I do. I feel that he reads the song because a song is a story and it's a story put to melody and you feel he sings a story. People often ask me, "How do you sing a song night after night, performance after performance?" I reply "I'm doing it to a different audience."

One of Elisabeth's mementoes from the first of her 1986 trips to New York was a telegram from Stephen Sondheim that she received on January 27. It said, simply, "Welcome back. You are indeed a Broadway Baby." A diary entry for November 19 that year confirms that Elisabeth met Britain's top theatre producer, Sir Cameron Mackintosh, at the New London Theatre to discuss the possibility of appearing in his forthcoming London production of Sondheim's *Follies*. Another diary entry confirms that on February 5, 1987, she met Sondheim at the Piccadilly Theatre. They wanted her to sing "Broadway Baby" in the show, but Elisabeth declined. By the time *Follies* opened at the Shaftesbury Theatre on July 21 she would have been eighty-three (but only admitting to seventy-eight); she explained that she would find eight performances a week too demanding. One can only speculate how disappointing this must have been for Sondheim and Mackintosh.

A diary entry for July 20 reveals that Elisabeth sent good-luck cards to several cast members, including Diana Rigg, Julia McKenzie, Dolores Gray, and Margaret Courtenay—who had been cast as Hattie Walker, the role intended for Elisabeth.

In 1989 Elisabeth gave an exquisite rendition of Sondheim's "Losing My Mind," from *Follies*, on her album *This Thing Called Love*. In 1990 she sang the role of the dowager Madame Armfeldt in a studio cast recording of *A Little Night Music*, with Sian Phillips as Desiree. Elisabeth's interpretation of "Liaisons" is softer and more reflective than Hermione Gingold's—closer to the latter's Broadway original than her fire-breathing West End re-creation. Hugh Miller described it in *Gay Times* (September 1990) as "a near perfect interpretation of a song that nicely combines melancholy with nostalgia."

In 1987 Elisabeth was the subject of the documentary film *Keeping Love Alive*, described by its makers as "a self portrait in words and songs." The format consisted of her own recollections of her career, told to an off-screen interviewer, and extracts from her one-woman show filmed at London's Almeida Theatre on May 21 and 22 before an invited audience. Elisabeth's repertoire included songs by Irving Berlin, Noël Coward, George Gershwin, and Cole Porter. The film was produced and directed by television producer Stephen Garrett and David Robinson, who was then the film critic for the London *Times*.

The distinguished film director Lindsay Anderson *(This Sporting Life, If . . . , O Lucky Man!)* was one of many friends, fans, and colleagues in the audience at the Almeida Theatre for the filming. In a private letter to Elisabeth, dated May 27, 1987, he wrote:

Dear Elisabeth Welch
Having had two wonderful evenings last week, on Thursday and Friday, at the Almeida, I feel I must write to thank you for the experience of such charm and artistry as one nowadays scarcely dare hope for. Your style and finesse and

lovely professionalism were a lesson to us all: but not painful as lessons can sometimes be, but deeply, refreshingly and movingly enjoyable. Thank you so much—and how good it is to know that it will all be there on film, to give pleasure to so many more, far and wide. You were and are and will always be absolutely terrific: what a joy fine art can be!
Thank you again—
Lindsay Anderson

A draft copy of Elisabeth's reply, dated June 5, 1987, has survived. She said:

Dear Lindsay Anderson
It was with overwhelming disbelief—my first reaction to your letter—then great joy when I re-read your words. Thank you very, very much! You made me very happy, and I can only wish that I live up to such praise for as long as time allows.
Most sincerely yours,
EW

On December 22, 1987, following screenings at the Edinburgh International Film Festival (August 22) and the London Film Festival (November 22), *Keeping Love Alive* was shown on British television. Critics were unanimous in their praise of Elisabeth. Said W. Stephen Gilbert in *The Independent* (December 22, 1987): "Welch is the last great exponent of the lyric (though she pays gracious tribute to Sinatra). She always sings the verse, and who else does that these days? The voice may lack tone and pitch now but no-one else graces the words with such wit, detachment, sensuality yet never a tinge of regret."

In a private letter to Elisabeth, dated December 23, 1987, Sir John Gielgud wrote:

Dear Liz
Your programme last night was such a delight. So amusing, dignified and elegant, just the right mixture and how splendid you looked in the red dress. I feel very privileged to have seen Piaf and Elena Gerhardt when she was in her late years, to say nothing of Mabel Mercer, whom I knew a little, and always went to see when I was in New York. I expect you knew her too. So lovely that you have repeated your earlier triumphs and gained, I am sure, a whole new audience of youngsters—and something of the sort has happened to me too. So the TV and cinema are certainly not to be despised! May our health and memory long hold out!
All love and congratulations—and no answer please.
As ever, John.

In an interview with the author on October 14, 1987, David Robinson revealed that as a child growing up in the 1940s he hadn't liked singers, "but for some reason I loved Elisabeth Welch." When he attended performances of her West End revues, *Tuppence Coloured, Oranges and Lemons,* and *Penny Plain,* Robinson was more interested in the "funny people," such as Joyce Grenfell and Max Adrian, "but Elisabeth fascinated me." In the early 1980s Robinson "rediscovered" Elisabeth in some of her one-woman shows:

> There is no doubt that Elisabeth's friend Bryan Hammond brought me back to her. Whenever she was performing he'd tell me about her and so gradually I became as keen as he was and, of course, I realised that here was someone absolutely extraordinary, wonderful, and unique. I rediscovered all my old love for her and found her even more fascinating because, instead of just *performing* the songs, she *acted* them. It was very important that she should be filmed. She gets more meaning out of a song than anybody else I know and she can sing a song that you've heard a hundred times and you really, truly hear it for the first time. In terms of personality and talent certainly I would put her with the great names of British musical theatre, such as Jack Buchanan, Noël Coward, and Gertrude Lawrence. She's the equal of any of them.
>
> I first met Elisabeth in 1983 when I interviewed her for *The Times* and when I approached her about making a film, she said: "Well, fine, but if you're going to do it you'd better do it quickly because I can do it now but who knows if I can do it in six months or a year's time." When you see Elisabeth on the stage she has a very special effect on an audience. She excites an audience and has an extraordinary rapport with them. She has a way of involving them in what she is doing and it's a wonderful experience just to be in an audience when Elisabeth is on stage. Our single aim in doing the film was to get as close as we could to this experience so that people who saw the film could get something of this experience. That's what we tried to do and it was very difficult to achieve. We felt that the way to do it was to impose ourselves as little as possible.
>
> The actual filming of the concerts was quite complicated. We had four cameras and each one was very carefully cued in advance. We aimed to get as close to Elisabeth as possible and put as little as possible between her and the audience. On the first night of filming she accepted what was happening. On the second night she was directing! She was absolutely in control. She'd say, "Right. Wait a minute. I'll start that song again," or ask "Why aren't the cameras there?" It was marvellous. She's incredibly professional and after all those years in the business she just knows her job through and through. No question about it.
>
> When she saw *Keeping Love Alive* for the first time at the Edinburgh Film Festival she did quite dislike some of the shots of herself. Nobody ever likes to see themselves on a big screen. I think that moment distressed her when she

saw it for the first time. To me, she's marvellous whatever way you look at her. I think she's beautiful from any angle. After the Edinburgh screening she was slightly shocked but she pulled herself together pretty quickly. I simply adore Irving Berlin's "When I Lost You" because it's such a simple song and it's performed at the only sad moment in the film. Elisabeth didn't have any sad stories to tell except the one about her father leaving. It's very hard to catch Elisabeth being sad. It's not in her nature but it's interesting because she often referred to that story but, until we got the camera on her, she'd never told it at that length, and so fully, and so very movingly. I felt that she was affected by telling it and so we just kept the camera on her. It is an extraordinary and moving moment in the film.

Off-stage Elisabeth is one of the most astounding personalities I have ever met. She has such a huge personality, warmth, intelligence, and understanding. She just has an enormous interest in other people. She's so shrewd about other people. She sees through any pretence.

Towards the end of the 1980s the record producer John Yap, of That's Entertainment Records, also "discovered" Elisabeth: "I was absolutely amazed at the clarity and the purity of the voice and I thought to myself 'God, this voice is still there.' So I got to know Lis and decided to make as many records as possible while the voice was as beautiful and pure as it was." Their association began with a celebration of Irving Berlin, to coincide with his centenary in 1988, and this was followed by a similar tribute to Jerome Kern. Other highlights included a collection of love songs called *This Thing Called Love* (1989), which featured John Lennon and Paul McCartney's "Yesterday"; Jule Styne, Betty Comden, and Adolph Green's "Long before I Knew You"; Cole Porter's "True Love"; and Noël Coward's "I'll Follow My Secret Heart." Stephen Sondheim's *A Little Night Music* followed in 1990.

In 1988 Elisabeth travelled—for the first time—to Australia, to appear in a version of her one-woman show called *She Shall Have Music* at Sydney's Footbridge Theatre. An unidentified reviewer in the *Australian Jewish Times* (February 12, 1988) revealed that on the opening night "there was as comprehensive and spontaneous a 'standing ovation' as we have ever seen, heard and been part thereof in our decades of Sydney theatre-going; and totally deserved." The reviewer added:

> She glows, she glitters, she shines from within, with the love of life showing, and the zest for living. She is equally and surprisingly at home in the romantic lilt of Coward's "I'll Follow My Secret Heart" and the bitter irony of Porter's "Miss Otis Regrets." She out-Marys Mary Martin in Rodgers and Hart's wickedly amusing "To Keep My Love Alive"; she evokes (does not mimic, for she is her own person) Piaf in *"La Vie en Rose"* and even Johnny Ray in "Such

a Night." . . . If there are better or more distinctive voices abroad, there is none used as an instrument with more consummate technique and artistry.

In October 1989 Elisabeth returned to New York to tumultuous acclaim for two concerts at the Weill Recital Hall, at Carnegie Hall, and *A Cabaret Concert: Sunday in New York* at Town Hall. These performances formed part of the first convention of The Mabel Mercer Foundation, an organisation founded by Donald Smith in 1985, a year after the death of the legendary chanteuse, to keep the late singer's memory—and the art of cabaret—alive.

By the 1990s Elisabeth had begun to take things easier, though she con-tinued to wow London audiences in occasional charity concerts, including *Cole Porter's Nymph Errant* (1989) for The Greater London Fund for the Blind, the *Cole Porter Centennial Gala* (1991) in aid of the Cancer Research Campaign, and *A Time to Start Living: A Celebration of the Great Elisabeth Welch* (1992), a World AIDS Day Gala (see "Concerts"). When she made an appearance in *A Glamorous Night with Evelyn Laye and Friends* on July 26, 1992, she used a pianist for accompaniment, not the orchestra, and reduced the huge London Palladium theatre to the intimacy of a nightclub. The au-dience gave her a standing ovation.

In 1992 Elisabeth made her final appearances in New York. Signed to make her debut at The Russian Tea Room on October 25, Elisabeth was also persuaded by her friend Bobby Short to sing in *A Gala Concert of Duke Elling-ton* at Saint Peter's Church and *Salute to Mae Barnes* at New York's Town Hall. The latter was part of the third Cabaret Convention presented by the Mabel Mercer Foundation. These performances were attended by Delilah Jackson, a fan of Elisabeth's. Delilah is also an avid researcher and historian as well as the owner of an extensive private collection of African American theatre memorabilia. In an interview with the author, she described those fi-nal appearances in New York:

> Miss Welch was a legend, a black woman who went to Europe and became a star. She reminded me of Dorothy Dandridge, radiant and always sparkling. She had a beautiful smile and was so full of fun. It was Revella Hughes who gave Miss Welch her start. They were in *Runnin' Wild* and a young girl was needed to sing "Charleston." Revella said "I know just the girl. She sings like an angel." Joe Attles told me he knew Miss Welch when they worked together in *Blackbirds of 1928*. He said she was always imitating Ethel Waters. At Bobby Short's programme for Duke Ellington I was waiting for Miss Welch at the stage door. She was delighted to see me, smiled and gave me a hug. Her song was one of the hits of the show, "Sophisticated Lady." There was a dancer there who knew Miss Welch from his stay in London in 1933, one of the Five Hot

Shots, a dance team in *Dark Doings.* I said to Miss Welch, "This dancer worked with you when he was young." She replied, "We were both young then." Mae Barnes was honoured at Town Hall. Miss Welch said she and Mae went to grade school together. So she sang at the programme. The audience went wild for her and gave her a standing ovation for three minutes. Town Hall was packed.

In her second appearance in BBC radio's *Desert Island Discs* (November 18, 1990) (see "Credits," "Radio"), Elisabeth informed the presenter, Sue Lawley, that the turning point in her career had been the 1930 "audition" for Irving Berlin, E. Ray Goetz, and Monty Woolley, which led to her being cast in *The New Yorkers* and singing Cole Porter's "Love for Sale." At the end of the programme she made the following revelation when asked what she would take to a desert island: "I'd take my Mama's photograph with me because I talk to her a lot. I just look at her and talk. I always keep her photograph by my bed. I like to feel her around." She also informed Lawley that she was happy to slow down and take things easy.

CHAPTER ELEVEN

~

Finale

A Bachelor Girl

On November 5, 1995, Elisabeth participated in *A Handful of Keys: A Tribute to Martin Smith* at the Prince Edward Theatre. Smith, a popular actor, singer, and composer, had died one year earlier, on November 5, 1994. All proceeds of the all-star gala were donated to Crusaid/West End Cares, Britain's National AIDS Fundraising Charity. Elisabeth declined to sing at the event but agreed to appear on stage to present the cheque. The audience gave her a rousing ovation.

Shortly afterwards one of Elisabeth's closest friends, Kenneth Partridge, discovered that she had taken to her bed. She had been turning away visitors, and when speaking to friends on the phone she gave no indication of her situation. Kenneth decided to intervene. With the consent of her brother John, who was living in New York, Kenneth persuaded Elisabeth to have a two-week "holiday" in Denville Hall, a retirement home for actors and actresses, situated on the outskirts of London in Northwood, Middlesex. Elisabeth never returned to Capener's Close. Denville Hall became her new home.

Not long after settling into Denville Hall, Elisabeth joined other residents on visitor's day on Sunday afternoon. As she sat comfortably in an armchair, minding her own business, a visitor came up to her and exclaimed, "I know who you are! You're Elisabeth Welch! You used to sing 'Stormy Weather.'" Elisabeth sat bolt upright and promptly replied, "My dear, I still do." Then

she launched into "Stormy Weather," from beginning to end, unaccompanied, while the startled visitor, staff, and other guests listened in admiration.
Even in retirement Miss Welch could stop the show.

On September 1, 1996, Elisabeth made her final television appearance, in
the Channel 4 documentary *Black Divas*. She had been filmed at Denville
Hall, on April 16, in conversation with her friend, critic and jazz singer
George Melly. During the conversation with Melly, Elisabeth sang "Stormy
Weather" one more time for the cameras; this was one of the highlights of
the programme. It was the last time the public would hear her sing.

Elisabeth's final public appearance took place at the London Palladium on
February 28, 1997, one day after her ninety-third birthday. Sir Cameron
Mackintosh had hoped to persuade her to appear on-stage in an all-star tribute to his friend Jack Tinker, the well-known *Daily Mail* theatre critic, who
had suddenly died from a heart attack at the age of fifty-eight. A frail Elisabeth declined to appear on stage, but she did leave Denville Hall (for the last
time) to watch the show from one of the boxes. During the tribute her presence was announced, and she happily gave a wave to the audience, which
was delighted and gave her a standing ovation. It was around this time that
she said: "I don't have a favourite period in my life. I enjoyed it all, absolutely. I have always liked people and so I can't hurt people, knowingly. Life
has been marvellous to me."

Every summer Elisabeth's younger brother John travelled from New York
to visit her at Denville Hall. He passed away at the age of ninety-two in New
York on July 4, 1999. He had been due to visit his sister again that summer.
When Elisabeth was informed about John's passing, she shed a tear and said,
"He was the baby. I'll never see him again." John's wife Elsie had passed away
in New York on January 13, 1972. Elisabeth's older brother, Edward, had died
at the age of seventy-six in New York on February 13, 1979, two days before
she started filming *The Tempest*. Edward's widow, Miriam, outlived Elisabeth
and became her only surviving relative, for neither Edward or John had fa-
thered any children.

Elisabeth passed away on July 15, 2003. Miles Kreuger, president of the Institute of the American Musical, a Los Angeles research library, told the *Los
Angeles Times* (July 19, 2003): "Elisabeth Welch wasn't just another singer;
she was a cultural icon, like Ella Fitzgerald is to this country. She could do
anything—she could sing jazz, she could sing popular music with the most
sweet and plaintive voice, and she had absolutely impeccable diction and
taste. In a recording career that began in 1928 and lasted into the 1990s her
voice was absolutely untouched by time."

Elisabeth's funeral service took place in The Chapel at Breakspear Crematorium near Denville Hall on July 21. The service was presided over by the Reverend Ian Wiseman, who brought warmth and intimacy to the proceedings. Between vintage Elisabeth Welch recordings, Moyra Fraser read three pieces of Shakespeare, Derek Granger quoted generous reviews, and her loyal friend Ned Sherrin spoke of Elisabeth's greatness. Her ashes were scattered around a pink rose blossom tree in the grounds of Denville Hall.

Some months after Elisabeth passed away, I found amongst her private papers a copy of a revealing article entitled "I Love Being a Bachelor Girl." This had been written by Elisabeth and published in an unidentified American journal. She had dated it December 1952. After describing some of the highlights of her career in Britain, she turned her attention to interracial marriage (then still against the law in a number of American states), the role of women, and her "bachelor girl" status:

I live a bachelor's existence and I love it. Not that I couldn't be married again. During the last twenty years of a busy, eventful life as a singer in London and Paris, I have had numerous proposals from the lowly as well as the high and mighty. It's just that I've lived alone so long that to change my way of life by bringing a husband again into it just doesn't sound too interesting. In fact, who would want to marry me anyway, even though I am considered the Josephine Baker of London's theatre, radio, television and night club world? Of course I believe in marriage but I definitely do not relish the seemingly popular habit of signing on a husband almost as often as signing a new contract. My interest in the subject of the bachelor girl stems from the fact that over the years, our numbers have increased to the point where there are enough of us to gang up on any group seeking to push us around. Among us, Negro and white alike are great numbers of eminently successful women and to name a few in America there are Zora Neale Hurston, the novelist; Dr. Mary McLeod Bethune, the eminent educator; Hattie McDaniel, the movie star; and, my very good friend, Ethel Waters. But my bachelorhood is not a state of belligerency that I assume when the question, "Why don't you marry?" comes up. Instead, it is a more than happy existence, one full of faith and confidence in myself and in which I can have the supreme satisfaction of achievement and of making other people happy. And as a bachelor girl for many years, I am not lonely for the company of men, for I have that—as much, if not more than many women, who are far younger but who do not, for certain reasons, attract men of the right calibre and background.

There are several perfectly valid reasons for bachelor women like me. The first is that we have well-defined ideas about ourselves that involve a sort of self-worship. This imparts a strong measure of self-reliance and enhances our personal value, at least to ourselves. When a woman is able to demonstrate to the world that she can support herself, make a name for herself and then on top of that, make a definite contribution to the culture and well-being of humanity, she most certainly is going to do quite a bit of sober reflection when it comes to giving up her independence for an uncertain life of cooking, making up beds and possibly raising children. . . . I am the product of an interracial marriage. Therefore, I consider such marriage natural; for love has no barriers and should not be hindered by laws. . . . But more important to me are the problems affecting women. This is a subject that crops up very often today. Women have now entered into fields which even up till pre-war were considered to be reserved for men only. I am sure that coloured women in America and elsewhere, in common with all other women, will make careers for themselves with the men, not as female freaks but as equal partners. My life as a career woman has been in general a very happy one. I've loved living alone all these years. I find that as a bachelor woman the comfort of my home is my great love, and it is to this great love that I always enjoy coming back, be it from a wonderful trip abroad, or a gay party, or just from a day's work. . . . See that you have a very comfortable bed, as lovely a bed as possible. For me, that was the first thing I chose for my flat. Make it as pretty as you can. Dress up for bed as you do for going out. Wear nice nighties or pyjamas. Have a choice, if possible, of bed-jackets and dressing gowns, and enjoy wearing them. You may be one of those odd people who hate staying in bed. If so, try and make yourself like it by making it your sanctuary . . . and you'll soon see just how enjoyable a bed can be—alone! Make your house your castle, whether you have lots to spend on it, or little. With that as background you can be happy.

And being happy you attract and gain friends. That's good. We all need friends. . . . All this sounds like good advice, doesn't it? You're right. It *is* good advice. I know, for I've lived life—not madly—but well! Yes, and I've enjoyed my life. Of course, I've had heartaches, depressions and tears, but my career has always pulled me through. My career has been my strength. My strength has grown from my independence. My independence developed because of my bachelor life, and my bachelor life is my FREEDOM.

CHAPTER TWELVE

~

Invisible Women: A Survey of Black Women in British Films

When Marianne Jean-Baptiste became the focus of media attention at the time of the Cannes Film Festival in 1997 it was not because she had landed a major role in a film but because she had made accusations of racism. Within months of receiving BAFTA (British Academy of Film and Television Arts), Golden Globe, and Oscar nominations for Mike Leigh's *Secrets and Lies,* the actress complained that she had been excluded from a celebration attended by Britain's newest film personalities. Simon Perry, chief executive of British Screen, had invited a group of young actors, including Emily Watson and Kate Winslet, to the festival, but there were no black actors on the list. In *The Guardian* (May 15, 1997) Marianne complained:

> When I was told that British Screen had invited a group of young actors out to Cannes, I just burst into tears because I thought this is so unfair. It was a snub. What more do they want? If you think about it, I made history. Not only was I the first black British woman to be nominated for an Oscar, I was the first black British person. I see myself as British and I want to be celebrated by Britain. . . . I don't want to sound like someone who has a chip on their shoulder. But if you keep quiet nothing will ever change and nothing will ever be done about it.

The story of black women in British cinema has always been one of invisibility, and yet those who have made an impression—such as Elisabeth Welch, Nina Mae McKinney, Cleo Laine, Shirley Bassey, Cassie McFarlane, Cathy Tyson, and Marianne Jean-Baptiste—are constantly "written out" of histories of film.

Elisabeth Welch's British screen career spanned over fifty years, from her 1934 debut to the 1987 documentary *Keeping Love Alive*. In 1989 she became the first—and only—performer to be recognised by America's Black Film-makers Hall of Fame for appearances in British films, which is a measure of her importance in British cinema history.

With the exception of Elisabeth, black women cabaret or stage stars made only rare appearances in British films of the 1930s, and these were usually "guest" appearances in musical sequences. They included the great American blues singer and composer Alberta Hunter in *Radio Parade of 1935* (1934), the British-born cabaret singer Mabel Mercer in *Everything Is Rhythm* (1936), and Jeni Le Gon, a talented American buck-and-wing, acrobatic, and "flash" dancer, in *Dishonour Bright* (1936). An exception was Nina Mae McKinney, known as "the Black Garbo." In 1935 she co-starred with Paul Robeson in *Sanders of the River*.

In the 1930s in Britain there was a lot of work for black chorus girls, especially in West End nightclubs and the popular *Blackbirds* revues, but there were only fleeting appearances in British films. In *London Melody* (1937), Anna Neagle—in a stunning white gown—sang "Jingle of the Jungle" with a group of scantily clad black chorines in the background.

During the war one of Britain's most distinguished stage and screen actresses, Flora Robson, "blacked up" to play Cleopatra's slave Ftatateeta in Gabriel Pascal's lavish screen version of George Bernard Shaw's *Caesar and Cleopatra* (1945), but Ftatateeta is nothing more than a grim, over-bearing savage. Occasionally a small acting role surfaced for a black actress. Thus, British cinema audiences saw—for the first and last time—Princess Kouka (from Sudan) as Paul Robeson's wife in *Jericho* (1937); Eseza Makumbi (from Uganda) as Robert Adams's sister in *Men of Two Worlds* (1946); Carmen Manley (from Jamaica) as Earl Cameron's wife in *Emergency Call* (1951); Vivienne Clinton (from Exeter) as Mary Kumalo in *Cry, the Beloved Country* (1952); child actresses Cleopatra Sylvestre in the Children's Film Foundation's *Johnny on the Run* (1953) and Marjorie Fender in the Norman Wisdom comedy *One Good Turn* (1954); Trinidadian calypso singer Lucille Mapp as one of the nurses in *No Time for Tears* (1957); and Shari as the prostitute in *Tiger Bay* (1959). But the most famous black woman in 1950s British cinema was the one cinemagoers never actually saw, other than as a corpse: the murder victim Sapphire Robbins in *Sapphire* (1959).

In the 1950s two exciting young singers, Cleo Laine (from London's Southall) and Shirley Bassey (from South Wales) burst onto the British music scene, but in spite of their popularity, they failed to make the transition to movie stardom. In fact, Laine had to wait until she was over seventy to play her first screen acting role, when she was given a supporting role in BBC television's *The Last of the Blonde Bombshells* (2000), starring Judi Dench. Though she was cast as a jazz singer, Laine could have given Dench a run for her money if she had been given a more substantial acting role. It shouldn't be forgotten that Laine made her acting debut on the London stage just a few months after Dench. In May 1958 she debuted at the Royal Court in *Flesh to a Tiger*, written by the Jamaican dramatist Barry Reckord. Despite critical acclaim (the *Daily Sketch* described her performance as an "astonishing debut"), Laine knew the score. In her autobiography she said, "I had to play the waiting game until a director came along who wanted me . . . except, of course, as an English rosebud." For several years, Laine did have a film career of sorts. In the "pop" musical *6.5 Special* (1958) she sang a jazz number, accompanied by her husband John Dankworth and his orchestra, and in Joseph Losey's *The Criminal* (1960) she sang (brilliantly) John Dankworth and Alun Owen's haunting "Thieving Boy" on the soundtrack. In 1963 she made an important—but overlooked—contribution to Joseph Losey's *The Servant*, starring Dirk Bogarde. The moody theme song, "All Gone," written by Harold Pinter (who also wrote the film's screenplay—his first for the cinema) and performed by Laine in various atmospheric John Dankworth arrangements, is possibly the first use of a song lyric as part of a script. Not only is it the film's warning of the gathering darkness surrounding two of its main characters, Susan (Wendy Craig) and Tony (James Fox), but it draws attention to Tony's growing emotional and possible sexual dependence on his man-servant, Barrett (Bogarde).

It took until 1996 for Shirley Bassey to make her first on-screen film appearance, when she played herself in *La Passione*, performing a camp cabaret waltz surrounded by gleaming red Ferraris. However, like Laine, Bassey has made important contributions to the soundtracks of British films. When the dynamic Bassey belted out the theme song to *Goldfinger* (1964) she became forever associated with the James Bond films and an integral part of their success. Bassey was known internationally as "The Goldfinger Girl." When she sang "Goldfinger" in Las Vegas in 1964, she was shocked by the audience's reaction. They were surprised to find a black woman singing the James Bond theme. They had never seen her and had assumed she was white.

Bassey sang on the soundtracks of two thrillers, *The Liquidator* (1966) starring Rod Taylor and *Deadfall* (1967) starring Michael Caine, before returning to Bond themes. Her sexy and teasing rendition of the title song to *Diamonds Are Forever* (1971) provided her with another show-stopping concert favourite, but she bowed out after her third Bond movie song, *Moonraker* (1979). The tradition of using black divas on the soundtracks of Bond movies has continued with Gladys Knight (*Licence to Kill*, 1989) and Tina Turner (*Goldeneye*, 1995).

Apart from *La Passione*, Bassey has never made an appearance on the big screen. The closest she got to movie stardom was as Nancy in *Oliver!* (1968), a screen version of Lionel Bart's popular stage musical based on Charles Dickens's novel *Oliver Twist*. She was the director Carol Reed's first choice for the role. Bassey was under consideration because she had had a hit in the British pop charts with her recording of Nancy's big number, "As Long As He Needs Me." Casting Bassey in such an important musical role on the screen would have been revolutionary in 1968, but there were problems. Robert F. Moss revealed in *The Films of Carol Reed* (1987) that the director's first choice for this part was Bassey, "but Columbia vetoed her because it was felt that a black Nancy would alienate [white] filmgoers in the American South." In *The Man Between: A Biography of Carol Reed* (1990), Nicholas Wapshott gave a different version: "Columbia vetoed the idea, believing that the murder of a black woman [at the hands of Bill Sikes] would cause unnecessary offence to American audiences, particularly to southern blacks."

Other black pop singers who appeared up in British films of this period included Millie, the Jamaican reggae singer, who performed her hit record "My Boy Lollipop" in *Swinging UK* (1964). Later that year Millie co-starred with Elisabeth Welch in *The Rise and Fall of Nellie Brown*, an enchanting musical specially written for television. In 1975 the flamboyant American soul diva Tina Turner appeared as the Acid Queen in *Tommy*. This was Ken Russell's overblown version of The Who's rock-opera about a deaf, dumb, and blind boy who becomes a pinball-playing messiah. Touching on adultery, sadism, male rape, and drug addiction, Turner's "turn" is horrible. The Acid Queen exists above a sleazy strip-joint run by Tommy's sleazier step-dad, Frank (Oliver Reed). With a red neon light constantly flashing, the scantily dressed, over-sexed Acid Queen, waving a syringe in the air, attacks the defenceless Tommy and introduces him to drugs. In her autobiography *I, Tina* (1986), Turner admitted she should have known better: "Then we came to my big scene, and this pair of twins walk in with a pink pillow—and there's this *huge* hypodermic needle on it! I was shocked—I didn't know anything about this. I said right out loud, 'My God, is this movie promoting drugs?' I don't know why I'm so naive about those things. I mean, even the name of my character—the Acid Queen—hadn't tipped me off. Ken Russell just laughed, though."

It is sad that Patricia Ngozi Ebigwei felt it necessary to anglicize her—much prettier—Nigerian name to Patti Boulaye in order to be accepted by the British public, but that's what she was expected to do in the 1970s. She won popularity and fame after a memorable debut on television's *New Faces* talent show in 1976, but she failed in her attempt to become Britain's answer to Diana Ross. Her appearance in *The Music Machine* (1979), released at the height of the disco craze, didn't help matters. It was vastly inferior to Hollywood's *Saturday Night Fever*, which it tried to copy. Camden Town's Music Machine discotheque was no substitute for New York's Studio 54. Another fine singer whose film career ended before it had barely begun was the Nigerian/British soulstress Helen Folasade Adu, popularly known as "Sade." In 1986 she appeared as the nightclub singer Athene in *Absolute Beginners*, but this musical version of Colin MacInnes's novel about life in 1950s Soho and Notting Hill was an expensive flop. Sade's film career sank faster than Patti Boulaye's.

In addition to these brief appearances by singers, the British film industry offered sexy slave girls in films like *Up Pompeii* (1971), an occasional vampire (Marsha Hunt in *Dracula AD 1972*), an occasional exotic superstar (Eartha Kitt in *Up the Chastity Belt*, 1972), and Minah Bird, the only major black starlet in British sex films. During this period more substantial roles were given to Glenna Forster-Jones in John Boorman's critically acclaimed *Leo the Last* (1969), Sheila Scott-Wilkinson in *The National Health* (1973) and Horace Ove's *Pressure* (1975), Esther Anderson (as Sidney Poitier's love interest) in *A Warm December* (1973), and Floella Benjamin in *Black Joy* (1977).

Hardly any British historical films acknowledged the existence of women of African descent. For instance, no one has attempted to film the life of Mary Seacole, the Jamaican nurse who was decorated by Queen Victoria for her work in the Crimean War. It was not until Shope Shodeinde was cast in *The Sailor's Return* (1978) that a black actress was given an opportunity to play a historical role. James Saunders based his script on the novella by David Garnett, first published in 1924. Set during the reign of Queen Victoria, it was within a very English tradition of doomed love stories (like those of Thomas Hardy); it told the story of a sailor (Tom Bell) who returns to his West Country home with an African wife (Shodeinde). Though well received at the 1978 Cannes, Karlovy Vary, and London Film Festivals, a distributor could not be found, and the expected cinema release never happened.

In 1986 Cathy Tyson won critical acclaim—and a BAFTA nomination—for her role as a prostitute in *Mona Lisa*. A few years later Tyson complained that nearly all the parts she was offered in the wake of her success involved her taking her clothes off. On a happier note, in the independent sector a new generation of black film-makers provided decent roles for black actresses. Menelik

Shabazz's *Burning an Illusion* (1981) gave newcomer Cassie McFarlane a fully rounded, complex character to play. McFarlane went on to receive the 1982 *Evening Standard* Film Award for Most Promising Newcomer, but in spite of this achievement, film roles eluded her. In the 1980s and 1990s young black British women began working as film-makers in the independent sector. These included Maureen Blackwood (*The Passion of Remembrance*, 1986), Martina Attille (*Dreaming Rivers*, 1988), and Ngozi Onwurah (*Welcome II the Terrordome*, 1995). However, though these films offered positive roles for black actresses, they coincided with some objectionable stereotypes in commercial cinema. These included Alphonsia Emmanuel's over-sexed girlfriend of Tony Slattery in Kenneth Branagh's comedy *Peter's Friends* (1992). By the end of the 1990s the only black female movie star in Britain was Scary Spice in *Spice Girls: The Movie*, but in 1998 Anjela Lauren Smith gave a striking portrayal in *Babymother* of an unmarried mother with aspirations to become a dance-hall queen. Although the film didn't propel her into movie stardom, Anjela gave a vibrant performance in this enjoyable melodrama, with songs and attitude. To achieve her ambition, the "babymother" dumps her "babyfather," steals his money, and sells her body to pay for an expensive session in a recording studio. Though *Babymother* had a black writer/director, Julian Henriques, reactions were mixed, especially in Britain's young black community.

It is a sad indictment of the British film industry that Elisabeth Welch has been the only black actress to achieve stardom. Still, in spite of her successes and her 1989 citation from America's Black Filmmakers Hall of Fame, Elisabeth was missing from an important tribute shortly after her death. In addition to such cinema legends as Katharine Hepburn, Bob Hope, Gregory Peck, Alan Bates, and John Schlesinger, 2003 saw the passing of Elisabeth. However, during the BAFTA awards ceremony on February 15, 2004, Elisabeth was omitted from a tribute to those who had passed away in the previous year. In a response to a letter of complaint from the author, BAFTA's chief executive, Amanda Berry, apologised: "You are right we should have included Elisabeth Welch in our televised obituary tribute. She had a distinguished movie career stretching six decades and definitely should have been there. We apologise for the omission."

~

Elisabeth Welch's Credits

Theatre

New York (1922–1986)

Liza (Daly's Theatre, November 27, 1922). Musical. EW as a Brown-Skin Vamp. With Gertrude Saunders.

Runnin' Wild (Colonial Theatre, October 29, 1923). Musical. EW as Ruth Little. With Adelaide Hall.

The Chocolate Dandies (Colonial Theatre, September 1, 1924). Musical. EW as Jessie Johnson. With Sissle and Blake, Amanda Randolph, Josephine Baker, and Valaida Snow.

Blackbirds of 1928 (Liberty Theatre, May 9, 1928). Revue. With Adelaide Hall, Bill Robinson, Aida Ward, and Cecil Mack Choir.

The New Yorkers (Broadway Theatre, December 8, 1930). Revue. In January 1931 EW replaced Kathryn Crawford as May.

Black Broadway (Town Hall, May 1, 1980). Revue. With Adelaide Hall, Honi Coles, John W. Bubbles, Edith Wilson, Bobby Short, Gregory Hines, and Nell Carter.

Jerome Kern Goes to Hollywood (Ritz Theatre, January 23, 1986). Revue. With Elaine Delmar, Liz Robertson, and Scott Holmes.

Paris (1929)

Blackbirds (Moulin Rouge, June 7, 1929). Revue. With Adelaide Hall.

London (1933–1985)

Dark Doings (Leicester Square Theatre, June 26, 1933). Revue.

Nymph Errant (Adelphi Theatre, October 6, 1933). Musical. EW as Haidee Robinson. With Gertrude Lawrence.

Glamorous Night (Theatre Royal, Drury Lane, May 2, 1935). Musical. EW as Cleo Wellington. With Ivor Novello and Mary Ellis.

Let's Raise the Curtain (Victoria Palace, September 28, 1936). Revue. With Florence Desmond.

It's in the Bag (Saville Theatre, November 4, 1937). Revue. With Doris Hare, Robert Ashley, Gene Sheldon, Benny Ross, and Sepha Treble.

No Time for Comedy (Haymarket Theatre, March 27, 1941). Comedy. EW as Clementine. With Rex Harrison, Diana Wynyard, and Lilli Palmer.

Sky High (Phoenix Theatre, June 4, 1942). Revue. With Hermione Baddeley, Hermione Gingold, Walter Crisham, and Naunton Wayne.

Arc de Triomphe (Phoenix Theatre, November 9, 1943). Musical. EW as Josephine. With Ivor Novello, Mary Ellis, and Peter Graves.

Happy and Glorious (London Palladium, October 3, 1944). Revue. With Tommy Trinder, Cairoli Brothers, Zoe Gail, and Debroy Somers and His Orchestra.

Tuppence Coloured (Lyric Theatre, September 4, 1947. Transferred to Globe Theatre, October 15, 1947). Revue. With Joyce Grenfell and Max Adrian.

Oranges and Lemons (Lyric Theatre, November 26, 1948. Transferred to Globe Theatre, January 26, 1949). Revue. With Diana Churchill and Max Adrian.

Penny Plain (St. Martin's Theatre, June 28, 1951). Revue. With Joyce Grenfell and Max Adrian.

Pay the Piper (Saville Theatre, December 21, 1954). Revue. With Elsie and Doris Waters.

The Crooked Mile (Cambridge Theatre, September 10, 1959). Musical. EW as Sweet Ginger. With Jack MacGowran and Millicent Martin.

Cindy-Ella (or *I Gotta Shoe*) (Garrick Theatre, December 17, 1962). Musical. EW as Mr. Smith, Esmee, Lovable, Fairy Godmammy, and Major Domo. With Cleo Laine, Cy Grant, and George Browne.

Cindy-Ella (revival) (Arts Theatre, December 23, 1963). Musical. With Cleo Laine, Cy Grant, and George Browne.

A Marvellous Party (Hampstead Theatre Club, December 30, 1970). Revue.

Pippin (Her Majesty's Theatre, October 30, 1973). Musical. EW as Berthe. With Northern J. Calloway, Patricia Hodge, Paul Jones, Diane Langton, and John Turner.

Cindy-Ella (revival) (Criterion Theatre, December 15, 1976). Musical. With Linda Lewis and Clarke Peters.

Aladdin (Lyric, Hammersmith, December 21, 1979). Musical. EW as Fatimah, a wise woman.

Jerome Goes to Hollywood (Donmar Warehouse Theatre, May 28, 1985). Revue. With David Kernan, Liz Robertson, and Elaine Delmar.

Kern Goes to Hollywood (Donmar Warehouse Theatre, July 22, 1985). Revue.

Blackpool (1938–1943)

All the Best (Opera House, June 1938). Revue.

We're All in It (Opera House, May 1943). Revue.

Guildford (1966–1974)

Night Is for Delight (Yvonne Arnaud Theatre, October 19, 1966). Revue.

The Sweetest Sounds (Yvonne Arnaud Theatre, September 6, 1971). Revue.

Now and Then (Yvonne Arnaud Theatre, May 6, 1974). Revue.

Films

1934   *Death at Broadcasting House*. Crime drama directed by Reginald Denham. Cast includes Ian Hunter, Austin Trevor, Mary Newland, Henry Kendall, Val Gielgud, Peter Haddon, Jack Hawkins, and Donald Wolfit. EW appears as herself with Ord Hamilton (piano) and Chappie D'Amato (guitar) and sings "Lazy Lady" with music and lyric by Ord Hamilton.

1936   *Soft Lights and Sweet Music*. Musical-comedy revue directed by Herbert Smith. Cast includes Ambrose and His Orchestra, Evelyn Dall, Western Brothers, Billy Bennett, Four Flash Devils, Turner Layton, Max Bacon and Wilson, Keppel, and Betty. EW appears as herself and sings "Yesterday's Thrill" with music by Len Challis and lyric by Sybil Wise.

1936   *Song of Freedom*. Drama directed by J. Elder Wills. Cast includes Paul Robeson, Esme Percy, George Mozart, Robert Adams, and Connie Smith. EW co-stars as Ruth Zinga and sings "Sleepy River" with Paul Robeson with music by Eric Ansell and lyric by Henrik Ege.

1936   *The Black Emperor*. A cut-down version of *Song of Freedom*, running approximately ten minutes, starring Paul Robeson and EW. A Moviepaks short distributed on 16 mm for home use only by the

Gaumont-British Library (later the Rank Film Library). The only known surviving print is held by the Ronald Grant Archive (Cinema Museum) in London.

1937 *Calling All Stars*. Musical-comedy revue directed by Herbert Smith. Cast includes Ambrose and his Orchestra, Carroll Gibbons and the Savoy Orpheans, Evelyn Dall, Max Bacon, Larry Adler, Billy Bennett, Flotsam and Jetsam. EW appears as herself in the "Harlem Holiday" (Cotton Club) sequence with Buck and Bubbles, Turner Layton, and the Nicholas Brothers and sings "Nightfall" with music by Benny Carter and lyric by Manny Kurtz.

1937 *Big Fella*. Musical directed by J. Elder Wills. Cast includes Paul Robeson, Eldon Grant, Roy Emerton, James Hayter, Lawrence Brown, and Eslanda Robeson. EW co-stars as Manda and sings two songs: "One Kiss" and "Harlem in My Heart" with music by Eric Ansell and lyrics by James Dyrenforth.

1937 *Over the Moon*. Comedy directed by Thornton Freeland and William K. Howard. Cast includes Merle Oberon, Rex Harrison, Ursula Jeans, Robert Douglas, Louis Borell, Zena Dare, and Peter Haddon. EW appears as a cabaret singer in Monte Carlo and sings "Red Hot Annabelle" with music by Mischa Spoliansky and lyric by Desmond Carter.

1938 *Around the Town*. Musical-comedy revue directed by Herbert Smith. Cast includes Vic Oliver, Irene Ware, and Finlay Currie. EW appears as herself. No further information available.

1942 *This Was Paris*. Spy drama directed by John Harlow. Cast includes Ann Dvorak, Ben Lyon, Griffith Jones, and Robert Morley. EW appears as a cabaret singer in Paris and sings "All This and Heaven Too" with music by Jimmy Van Heusen and lyric by Eddie DeLange.

1942 *Alibi*. Crime drama directed by Brian Desmond Hurst. Cast includes Margaret Lockwood, Hugh Sinclair, James Mason, Raymond Lovell, and Hartley Power. EW appears as a cabaret singer in Paris and sings two songs: "Stars in Your Eyes" (Spanish title: "Mar") with music by Gabriel Ruiz and English lyric by Desmond Carter, and "Chez Moi" with music by Paul Misraki and English lyric by Bruce Sievier from the French lyric of Jean Feline.

1944 *Fiddlers Three*. Musical-comedy directed by Harry Watt. Cast includes Tommy Trinder, Sonnie Hale, Frances Day, Mary Clare, Ernest Milton, Diana Decker, and Francis L. Sullivan. EW is featured as Thora, handmaiden to Poppae, and sings "Drums in My Heart" with music by Mischa Spoliansky and lyric by Diana Morgan.

1945 *Dead of Night.* Supernatural drama. EW is featured as Beulah, the owner of Chez Beulah, a Paris nightclub, in *The Ventriloquist's Dummy* segment with Michael Redgrave and Hartley Power. She sings "The Hullalooba," written and composed by Anna Marly, and accompanied by Frank Weir and His Sextet.

1946 *Television Is Here Again.* Documentary directed by Philip Dorte. EW appears as herself and sings a medley of "St. Louis Blues" with music and lyric by W. C. Handy and "Stormy Weather" with music by Harold Arlen and lyric by Ted Koehler accompanied by Debroy Somers and His Band.

1946 *Coco and the Bear/Coco the Angler,* etc. Advertising cartoons made by Gaumont-British Animation, directed by David Hand. EW provided the voice of the Negro boy Coco.

1960 *Our Man in Havana.* Comedy directed by Carol Reed. Cast includes Alec Guinness, Maureen O'Hara, and Noël Coward. EW appears briefly, billed on the cast list as "Beautiful Woman."

1960 *Cleopatra.* Drama directed by Rouben Mamoulian. Cast includes Elizabeth Taylor, Peter Finch, Stephen Boyd, and Harry Andrews. EW was featured as Cleopatra's handmaiden before filming was abandoned.

1971 *Girl Stroke Boy.* Comedy directed by Bob Kellett. Cast includes Clive Francis, Peter Straker, Michael Hordern, and Joan Greenwood. EW appears briefly as Mrs. Delaney, Peter Straker's mother.

1978 *Revenge of the Pink Panther.* Comedy directed by Blake Edwards. Cast includes Peter Sellers, Dyan Cannon, and Burt Kwouk. EW appears briefly as the brothel owner Mrs. Wu.

1979 *Arabian Adventure.* Children's adventure directed by Kevin Connor. Cast includes Christopher Lee, Milo O'Shea, Oliver Tobias, Emma Samms, Puneet Sira, Peter Cushing, Capucine, and Mickey Rooney. EW appears briefly as the Beggarwoman.

1979 *The Tempest.* Drama directed by Derek Jarman. Cast includes Heathcote Williams, Toyah Willcox, Jack Birkett, Karl Johnson, David Meyer, Peter Bull, Neil Cunningham, Richard Warwick, Ken Campbell, and Christopher Biggins. EW appears as a Goddess and sings "Stormy Weather" with music by Harold Arlen and lyric by Ted Koehler.

1987 *Empire of the Sun.* War drama directed by Steven Spielberg. Cast includes Christian Bale and John Malkovich. EW's 1940 recording of "These Foolish Things/A Nightingale Sang in Berkeley Square" is heard on the soundtrack.

1987 *Keeping Love Alive.* Documentary directed by Stephen Garrett and David Robinson. EW is featured as herself in "a portrait in words and songs." Includes extracts from *Song of Freedom*, *Over the Moon*, *Television Is Here Again* and *The Tempest.*

Television

The following is a partial list of Elisabeth Welch's many appearances on British television from 1936 to 1996. Most of the information has been collated from the *Radio Times* and *TV Times*, her scrapbooks and diaries, and several personality files held in the BBC's Written Archives.

Unless otherwise stated (ITV, Channel 4, and one American production), all of the following transmissions were produced by the BBC (British Broadcasting Corporation).

Titles of plays are highlighted in bold, followed by the name of character Elisabeth portrayed.

With the exception of her two appearances in *The Royal Variety Performance* and four appearances in the talk show *Wogan*, "first appearance" is indicated after a title to avoid repetition where further appearances followed in a series. For example, Elisabeth made over twenty appearances in *Play School* from 1966 to 1974, but only the first is listed.

Though everything from *Song by Song by Lorenz Hart* (1978) exists in various British television archives, very few appearances by Elisabeth *before* 1978 have survived. At the time of writing, only the following programmes have been located: *Music for You* (BBC May 16, 1956); *Sunday-Night Theatre: Mrs. Patterson* (BBC June 17, 1956); *Play of the Week: The Rise and Fall of Nellie Brown* (Anglia, December 28, 1964); *Not So Much a Programme, More a Way of Life* (BBC March 7, 1965), in which she sings "Feathers for Mine" with Cleo Laine; *BBC-3* (BBC February 26, 1966), in which she sings "In Old Barbados"; *Plunder* (BBC April 9, 1966), in which she sings "Stormy Weather"; *The Long Cocktail Party* (BBC April 23, 1966); *Play School* (BBC June 13, 1966); and *Play School* (BBC April 21, 1969).

1936–1937	"light music items"
1938	*Making a Gramophone Record*
1939	*Elisabeth Welch in Songs* (first appearance)
1949	*Oranges and Lemons*
1949	*Tuppence Coloured*
1950	*Light and Shade*
1950	*Kaleidoscope* (first appearance)

1950	*Starlight* (first appearance)
1951	*All the Fun of the Fair*
1952	*Penny Plain*
1953	*The 1953 Radio Show*
1954	*Come Dancing*
1954	*Salute to A.P.*
1954	**No Time for Comedy** (Clementine)
1955	*Limelight*
1955	*Face the Music*
1955	*Top Town*
1955	*Isn't It Romantic?*
1955	*Music for You*
1955	*Laurier Lister's Late Show* (first appearance) (ITV)
1956	**Mrs. Patterson (Sunday-Night Theatre)** (Bessie Bolt)
1956	*Joyce Grenfell Requests the Pleasure* (first appearance)
1956	*Ivor Novello*
1957	*The Fred Emney Show*
1957	*Those Wonderful Shows*
1957	*Pleasure Boat*
1957	*Alan Melville Takes You from A–Z*
1957	*Me, the Night & the Music*
1957	**The Grass Harp (Play of the Week)** (ITV) (Catherine Creek)
1958	*Tell the Truth* (ITV)
1958	*Hotel Imperial* (ITV)
1958	*The Henry Hall Show*
1959	*This Is Your Life* (Tommy Trinder)
1959	*Tonight* (first appearance)
1960	**The Facts of Life (Somerset Maugham Stories)** (ITV) (Night-club singer)
1960	*Late Night Extra* (ITV)
1960	*The Ivor Novello Awards*
1960	*Summer Fair* (ITV)
1961	*Godfrey Winn's Birthday Honours* (ITV)
1962	**The Brockenstein Affair** (Corinne)
1964	**Crane (Epitaph for a Fat Woman)** (ITV) (Assunta)
1964	**The Rise & Fall of Nellie Brown (Play of the Week)** (ITV) (Nellie Brown/Lillabelle Astor)
1965	*Not So Much a Programme, More a Way of Life*
1966	*Late Night Line Up*
1966	**Take a Sapphire** (Carlotta Joaquina)

1966	BBC-3
1966	*Going for a Song* (first appearance)
1966	*Plunder*
1966	*The Long Cocktail Party*
1966	*Play School* (first appearance)
1966	*I Gotta Shoe* or *Cindy-Ella*
1967	*Before the Fringe* (first appearance)
1967	**The Moon & Sixpence (Play of the Month)** (Tiare Johnson)
1968	*Jackanory* (first appearance)
1968	*Tickertape* (ITV)
1972	**The Man Who Came to Dinner (Hallmark Hall of Fame)** (USA)
1973	*Looks Familiar* (ITV)
1974	*This Is Your Life* (Jimmy Jewel) (ITV)
1978	*Song by Song by Lorenz Hart* (ITV)
1978	*Paul Robeson*
1979	*The Royal Variety Performance* (ITV)
1980	*Song by Song by Cole Porter* (ITV)
1981	*Joyce Grenfell: 1910–1979*
1983	*Here and Now* (ITV)
1983	*Black on Black* (C4)
1983	*A Plus* (ITV)
1984	*Royal Academy Summer Exhibition*
1984	*The Time of Your Life* (Anna Neagle)
1985	*This Is Your Life* (Johnny Johnson) (ITV)
1985	*Wogan*
1985	*This Is Your Life* (Elisabeth Welch) (ITV)
1985	*The Royal Variety Performance* (ITV)
1986	*Good Morning Britain* (ITV)
1986	*Wogan*
1986	*Getting On* (ITV)
1987	*Keeping Love Alive* (C4)
1988	*Wogan*
1989	*Variety Club Awards*
1990	*Wogan*
1990	*This Is Your Life* (Evelyn Laye) (ITV)
1992	*Without Walls* (For Love or Money) (C4)
1992	*Black and White in Colour* (Part 1)
1994	*A Night with Derek* (C4)

1995   *This Is Your Life* (Ned Sherrin)
1996   *Black Divas* (C4)

Radio

The following is a partial list of Elisabeth Welch's numerous appearances on British radio from 1933 to 1994. Most of the information has been found in her scrapbooks and diaries, as well as several personality files held in the BBC's Written Archives.

All of the following broadcasts were produced by the BBC (British Broadcasting Corporation) and, from 1967, abbreviations are as follows: R2 (Radio 2) and R4 (Radio 4).

Titles of plays are highlighted in bold, followed by the name of the character Elisabeth portrayed.

Very few of Elisabeth's radio appearances have survived. The following is a partial list of BBC Sound Archive holdings featuring Elisabeth: *Monday Night at Eight* (1940), *The Adventures of the Black Girl in Her Search for God* (1944), *The Princess Zoubaroff* (1962), *Back to Methuselah* (1966), edited extracts from an interview in *Home This Afternoon* (1966), edited extracts from an interview in *PM* (1970), *Final Curtain: Cockie (The Impresarios)* (1974), *Celebration (Paul Robeson)* (1974), *Valmouth* (1975), *Portrait of Piaf* (1976), *The Leading Ladies* (1977), *A Real Gentleman (Roy Plomley)* (1985), *In with the Old!* (1986), and *Desert Island Discs* (1990). The British Library's Sound Archive holdings include *Theatre Memories: Elisabeth Welch* (an interview with Peter Williams recorded on January 26, 1982) and a BBC Transcription of *The Wavendon Festival: Elisabeth Welch* (a twenty-eight-minute excerpt from a concert recorded at The Stables in Wavendon in 1971).

1933   *C. B. Cochran Presents*
1933   *Soft Lights and Sweet Music* (first appearance)
1934   *A Charity Affair*
1934   *Henry Hall's Guest Night*
1934   *Variety*
1935   *I've Got to Have Music*
1935   *Henry Hall's Jubilee Guest Night*
1935   *Jubilee Gala*
1935   *Gala Variety*
1936   *Molasses Club*
1936   *Tone and Colour*

1937   *Songs You Might Never Have Heard*
1937   *Monday at Seven*
1938   *Band Wagon*
1939   **Glamorous Night** (Cleo Wellington)
1939   *Brief Interlude*
1939   *Let's Keep It Dark*
1940   *Monday Night at Eight*
1940   *Rhapsody in Black*
1941   *West Indian Party*
1941   **No Time for Comedy (Starlight)** (Clementine)
1941   *American Eagle Club*
1941   *Calling the West Indies*
1942   *Australian Magazine*
1942   *Your Company Is Required*
1942   *Yours for a Song*
1942   *Let's Get Acquainted*
1943   *The Stars Come Out at Night*
1943   *African Starlight*
1943   *Vaudeville of 1943*
1943   *Take It from Here*
1944   *Band Call*
1944   **Broadway Slave** (Roxie Russell)
1944   *Atlantic Spotlight*
1944   *Vaudeville of 1944*
1944   **The Adventures of the Black Girl in Her Search for God** (the Black Girl)
1944   *Calling Gibraltar*
1944   *Here's Wishing You Well Again*
1944   *Worker's Playtime*
1944   *To Town on Two Pianos*
1944   *Over Here*
1945   *All Join In*
1945   *Short and Sweet*
1945   *Happy and Glorious* (excerpts)
1945   *The Stars Come Out*
1945   *Starlight*
1946   *Party Pieces*
1946   *Variety Bandbox*
1946   *Caribbean Carnival*
1946   *Easy to Remember*

1946   A Village in London
1948   I Like It Here (Woman's Hour)
1950   Music Hall
1950   Variety Fanfare
1951   Henry Hall's Guest Night
1951   Radio Parade
1951   Limelight
1951   Festival Parade
1951   Christmas Parade
1952   Desert Island Discs
1952   The Music Goes Round
1952   Home at Eight
1952   Star Show
1955   **Cry, the Beloved Country** (Gertrude Kumalo)
1955   Myself and Music
1956   Stanley Baxter Takes the Mike
1957   **Cindy-Ella** or **I Gotta Shoe** (Esmee)
1958   The Ivor Novello Story
1958   **Under the Sun** (Miss 'Gatha)
1959   The Tune and the Memory (Woman's Hour)
1960   On Stage, Everybody!
1962   **The Princess Zoubaroff** (Mrs. Blanche Negress, a novelist)
1964   **Trouble in Mind (The Negro in America)** (Wiletta)
1966   **Back to Methuselah** (The Negress)
1966   Home This Afternoon
1966   Elisabeth Welch
1970   PM (R4)
1974   Final Curtain: Cockie (The Impresarios) (R2)
1974   Celebration (Paul Robeson) (R4)
1975   **Valmouth (The Monday Play)** (R4) (Mrs. Yajnavalkya)
1976   Portrait of Piaf (R2)
1977   The Leading Ladies (R2)
1979   Ivor Novello: The Romantic (R2)
1979   Dance Band Days (R2)
1982   Woman's Hour (R4)
1983   **God in the Water (Afternoon Theatre)** (R4) (Madam Zenobia)
1985   A Real Gentleman (Roy Plomley tribute) (R4)
1985   Kenneth Alwyn (R2)
1986   **In with the Old!** (R2) (Miss Maude Kemble)
1987   Loose Ends (R4)

1988   *An Evening with Cole Porter* (R2)
1989   *Sweet and Low-Down* (R4)
1989   *Here's to the Next Time* (Henry Hall tribute) (R2)
1989   *Memories of You* (R2)
1990   *Desert Island Discs* (R4)
1992   *Steve Ross and Friends* (R2)
1992   *Myself When Young* (R2)
1992   *Woman's Hour* (R4)
1993   *Star Quality* (R2)
1993   *Salutations* (Leslie "Hutch" Hutchinson) (R2)
1993   *Christmas at the Ritz* (R4)
1994   *Black in the West End* (final appearance, interviewed by Stephen Bourne about Florence Mills) (R2)

Elisabeth Welch's *Desert Island Discs*
February 26, 1952, with Roy Plomley
1. Cole Porter's "Begin the Beguine"
2. Noël Coward's "I'll Follow My Secret Heart"
3. Johann Strauss's "Emperor Waltz"
4. Ravel's "Cat Duet" from *L'Enfant et les Sortileges*
5. Gracia de Triana's "Rincon de Espagne" (Corner of Spain)
6. Puccini's "In Questa Reggia" from *Turandot*, sung by Eva Turner
7. "La Golandrina" (Serradell, arranged by Melachrino)
8. Ivor Novello and Christopher Hassall's "Fold Your Wings" from *Glamorous Night*, sung by Mary Ellis and Trefor Jones

November 18, 1990, with Sue Lawley
1. Stephen Sondheim's "Broadway Baby" from *Follies*, sung by Elaine Stritch
2. Vernon Duke and E. Y. Harburg's "April in Paris," sung by Cleo Laine
3. Richard Rodgers and Lorenz Hart's "Little Girl Blue," sung by Mabel Mercer
4. Noël Coward's "A Marvellous Party," sung by Beatrice Lillie
5. Ivor Novello and Christopher Hassall's "Waking or Sleeping" from *Arc de Triomphe*, sung by Mary Ellis
6. Dave Barbour, Peggy Lee, and Willard Robison's "Don't Smoke in Bed," sung by Peggy Lee
7. Peter Sarstedt's "Where Do You Go To, My Lovely?" sung by Peter Sarstedt
8. Cole Porter's "Just One of Those Things," sung by Frank Sinatra
Book: *Who's Who in the Theatre*
Luxury object: Mama's photograph

Concerts

Elisabeth participated in many all-star galas and her one-woman show, mostly for charity. The following is a partial list of her appearances in London, Brighton, Bristol, Guildford, Newcastle, Oxford, Wavendon, New York, Los Angeles, Australia, and Russia from 1969 to 1993.

London

1969 (December 16) A Talent to Amuse (Phoenix Theatre) to honour Mr. Noël Coward on the occasion of his seventieth birthday and to aid the Combined Theatrical Charities

1970 (October 4) A Tribute to George Gershwin (Greenwich Theatre) a gala evening in aid of the Greenwich Theatre and the Wavendon Allmusic Plan

1971 (April 4) Ladies Night (Greenwich Theatre) in aid of the Greenwich Theatre and the Wavendon Allmusic Plan

1974 (August 4) A Galaxy of Stars (Theatre Royal, Drury Lane) in aid of the Tower Victims Fund

1976 (March 21) Kathy Stobart Quintet with Elisabeth Welch (Theatre Royal, Stratford East)

1976 (May 4) guest appearance at the British Music Hall Society (Horse Shoe Hotel)

1978 (December 17) Tonight at 8.30 (Royal Opera House, Covent Garden) a performance for the Friends of Covent Garden Opera

1979 (May 6) Fall In, the Stars (London Palladium) in aid of The Army Benevolent Fund (Children's Section)

1979 (June 23) Dance Band Days (Royal Festival Hall)

1979 (July 23 & 30) Elisabeth Welch in Cabaret (Country Cousin)

1979 (October 7) The Story of the Lyric (Lyric Theatre, Hammersmith) a special private performance for friends and patrons of the Lyric Theatre

1979 (November 26) Royal Variety Performance (Theatre Royal, Drury Lane)

1980 (April 20) The Gallery First-Nighters' Club Tribute to Evelyn Laye (Europa Hotel)

1981 (October 4) Elisabeth Welch in Cabaret (Company Restaurant and Piano Bar)

1982 (May 26 to 28) The Incomparable Elisabeth Welch (Riverside Studios)

1982 (June 19) Elisabeth Welch in Cabaret (Verrey's Restaurant)

1982   (June 23) *Elisabeth Welch in Cabaret* (Royal Academy of Art) private
event
1982   (August 15) *Images of Youth* (Round House) in aid of the Youth Training Fund
1982   (November 14) *An Evening with Elisabeth Welch* (Lyric Theatre, Hammersmith)
1984   (April 1) *Noël Coward: A Theatrical Celebration* (Theatre Royal,
Drury Lane) for The Noël Coward Charitable Trust and The Actors'
Charitable Trust
1984   (June 14) *Elisabeth Welch in Cabaret* (Carlton Club) a private event
in aid of The Arthritis and Rheumatism Council
1985   (January 20) *Gala: A Tribute to Joyce Grenfell* (Aldwych Theatre) to
benefit the Joyce Grenfell Centre and Festival
1985   (April 28) *All on an April Evening* (London Palladium) for The Cancer Research Campaign
1985   (May 6) *Paul Robeson Memorial Concert* (Queen Elizabeth Hall)
1985   (July 30) *The "Not Forgotten" Association* (Buckingham Palace Garden Party)
1985   (August 9) *Film Music Night at the Pops* (Barbican)
1985   (September 1) *A Tribute to Sir Michael Redgrave* (Old Vic)
1985   (September 15) *Show People* (Donmar Warehouse) a benefit for the
Terrence Higgins Trust
1985   (October 29) *Halley's Comet Royal Gala* (Wembley Conference
Centre)
1985   (November 25) *Royal Variety Performance* (Theatre Royal, Drury
Lane)
1986   (July 19) *Daily Mail/LSO Summer Pops: Transatlantic Night* (Barbican)
1986   (August 1 to 17) *Elisabeth Welch in Concert* (Donmar Warehouse)
1987   (February 27) *Elisabeth Welch in Concert* (Richmond Theatre)
1987   (March 14) *George Gershwin 50th Anniversary Concert* (Royal Festival
Hall)
1987   (April 12) *Will Aid: Action against AIDS Presents a Star-Studded Celebration of Shakespeare* (Sadler's Wells Theatre) an international AIDS
Day event
1987   (May 18 to 20) *Elisabeth Welch in Concert* (Almeida Theatre)
1987   (December 6) *"All I Want Is a Room Somewhere": A Dance Spectacular* (Sadler's Wells Theatre) in aid of the United Nations International Year of Shelter for the Homeless

1988   (March 27) *AWA Gala Benefit* (Adelphi Theatre) for the Arab Women's Association Orphans' Fund

1988   (March 27) *Sunday With Sondheim* (Shaftesbury Theatre) in aid of The Alan Page Heart Foundation and the Terrence Higgins Trust

1988   (April 17) *A Cavalcade of Coward* (Piccadilly Theatre) for the Terence Higgins Trust and Frontliners

1988   (June 7) *Rhapsody in Blue: Rambert Royal Gala Performance* (Sadler's Wells Theatre)

1988   (June 14) *Elisabeth Welch in Concert* (Bloomsbury Theatre)

1988   (August 7) *Benny Green and His Ladies* (Open Air Theatre, Regent's Park)

1988   (September 14) *The Music of Cole Porter* (Royal Festival Hall)

1988   (October 23) *Sundays at the Playhouse: Elisabeth Welch in Concert* (Playhouse Theatre) an AIDS fundraising performance, all proceeds donated to the Crusaid Haven Project

1988   (November 13) *A Memorial to the Victims of Stalin*: rally and concert (Adelphi Theatre) all proceeds to be presented to Professor L. A. Ponomarlov for the Public Council for the Memorial to the Victims of Stalin's Repression, USSR

1989   (April 23) *A Gala Late Joys* (The Players' Theatre at the Duchess Theatre)

1989   (May 21) *Cole Porter's Nymph Errant in Concert* (Theatre Royal, Drury Lane) in aid of The Greater London Fund for the Blind

1990   (March 4) *Perestroika: A Tribute and Concert in Memory of Gerry Healey* (Adelphi Theatre) proceeds to Symposium 1990

1990   (March 25) *Cook's Tour: A Musical Tribute to Ray Cook* (Shaftesbury Theatre) for Crusaid and Terrence Higgins Trust

1990   (June 5) *We Like Ike: A Musical Tribute* (Royal Festival Hall) a celebration of Dwight D. Eisenhower's centennial

1990   (July 22) *Magic of the Musicals* (Royal Festival Hall)

1990   (August 16) *LSO Summer Pops: Bewitched, Bothered, and Bewildered* (Barbican)

1991   (June 16) *Cole Porter Centennial Gala* (Prince Edward Theatre) in aid of The Cancer Research Campaign

1992   (July 26) *A Glamorous Night with Evelyn Laye and Friends* (London Palladium)

1992   (December 6) *A Time to Start Living: A Celebration of the Great Elisabeth Welch* (The Lyric Theatre, Shaftesbury Avenue) a World AIDS Day Gala

1992 (December 8) The "Not Forgotten" Association Christmas Party (Riding School, The Royal Mews, Buckingham Palace)
1993 (May 16) Mad about the Boy: A Star Studded Tribute to Noël Coward (The Lyric Theatre, Shaftesbury Avenue) a charity gala in aid of London Lighthouse, a centre for people facing the challenge of AIDS

Brighton
1971 (February 14) Gershwin Remembered (Gardner Centre) in aid of the Gardner Arts Centre
1976 (September 19) I Gotta Shoe (Gardner Centre)
1979 (September 30) 1969–1979 Tenth Anniversary Gala Performance (Gardner Centre) inaugurating a general fund-raising and sponsorship campaign on behalf of the Gardner Arts Centre
1984 (May 8) Elisabeth Welch in Cabaret: Brighton Festival (Old Ship Hotel)
1988 (May 12) The Irving Berlin Floor Show: Brighton Festival (Sallis Benney Theatre)
1989 (May 8) The George Gershwin Floor Show: Brighton Festival (Gardner Centre)

Bristol
1983 (March 13) Fall In, the Stars: A Gala Variety Show (Bristol Hippodrome) in aid of The Army Benevolent Fund

Guildford
1979 (April 29) A Gala Performance (Yvonne Arnaud Theatre) in aid of the Mount Alvernia Development Trust

Newcastle
1970 (October 10) Gershwin Gala: Newcastle Festival (City Hall)

Oxford
1991 (June) Oxford Playhouse Benefit Gala (Oxford Playhouse)

Wavendon (The Stables)
1970 (May 30 & July 5) Gershwin Gala: Wavendon Festival
1971 (May 31) A Marvellous Party
1976 (June 13) An Evening with Ned Sherrin/I Gotta Shoe
1976 (July 10) Kathy Stobart Quintet with Elisabeth Welch
1980 (December 7) Thank You, Joyce
1981 (March 29) Elisabeth Welch in Concert

1986   (December 3) *Elisabeth Welch in Concert*
1990   (July 1) *A Gala Evening of Noël Coward and Cole Porter* in aid of the All Saints Church, Emberton, Restoration Appeal

New York

1986   (March 20 to April 13) *Elisabeth Welch: Time to Start Living* (Lucille Lortel Theatre)
1986   (March 23) *In Living Color* (Carnegie Hall) a "Pops" benefit for the New York City Gay Men's Chorus
1989   (October 18 & 19) *Cabaret Comes to Carnegie: Elisabeth Welch in Cabaret* (Weill Recital Hall, Carnegie Hall) part of the first Cabaret Convention presented by The Mabel Mercer Foundation
1989   (October 22) *A Cabaret Concert: Sunday in New York* (Town Hall) part of the first Cabaret Convention presented by The Mabel Mercer Foundation
1991   (June 9) *The Cole Porter 100th Birthday Celebration* (Carnegie Hall)
1992   (October 22) *A Gala Concert of Duke Ellington* (Saint Peter's Church)
1992   (October 23) *Salute to Mae Barnes* (Town Hall) part of the third Cabaret Convention presented by The Mabel Mercer Foundation
1992   (October 25) *Cabaret at the Russian Tea Room* (The Russian Tea Room)

Los Angeles

1985   (October 21) *Jerome Kern: A Centennial Celebration* (Samuel Goldwyn Theatre, Academy of Arts and Motion Picture Arts and Sciences)

Richmond, Virginia

1986   (September 26 to 28) *Elisabeth Welch: Time to Start Living* (Theatre IV)

Australia

1988   (February 4 to 27) *She Shall Have Music: The Music, Career and Memories of Elisabeth Welch* (Footbridge Theatre, Sydney)

Russia

1990   (October Hall, Leningrad) to raise funds for rebuilding the Russian Theatre Workers' Union

Discography

Unless otherwise stated, the following titles were all recorded in London. Only the month and year of the recording are given.

Singles (78 rpm)

July 1928, "Diga Diga Do" (New York)

July 1928, "Doin' the New Low-Down" (New York)

March–April 1933, "Stormy Weather" (Paris)

March–April 1933, "Crying for Love" (Paris)

October 1933, "Solomon"

November 1933, "Silver Rose" (in C. B. Cochran Medley)

February 1934, "Soft Lights and Sweet Music Medley Pts. 1 & 2"

April 1934, "Soft Lights and Sweet Music Medley Pts. 3 & 4"

April 1935, "Far Away in Shanty Town"

April 1935, "The Girl I Knew"

May 1936, "I Still Suits Me" (duet with Paul Robeson)

May 1936, "Sleepy River" (duet with Paul Robeson)

June 1936, "I Gotta Go"

June 1936, "When Lights Are Low"

October 1936, "Poor Butterfly"

October 1936, "Drop in the Next Time You're Passing"

October 1936, "The Man I Love"

October 1936, "That's How the First Song Was Born"

July 1937, "Harlem in My Heart"

July 1937, "One Kiss"

January 1938, "Gershwin Medley Pts. 1–4"

October 1940, "These Foolish Things/A Nightingale Sang in Berkeley Square"

October 1940, "The Nearness of You"

October 1940, "Much More Lovely"

October 1940, "And So Do I"

December 1943, "Dark Music"

September 1951, "Stay Close to People"

September 1951, "Thanks for Understanding"

September 1951, "Alibis"

September 1951, "December Road"

November 1951, "Hold Me, Thrill Me, Kiss Me"

November 1951, "Until"

Singles (45 rpm)
February 1979, "Stormy Weather"
July 1979, "You're Blasé"

Long-Playing Records and Compact Discs
August 1959, *The Crooked Mile* (cast recording). Available on CD
May 1962, *Carmen Jones* (cast recording). Available on CD
September 1963, *Cindy-Ella or I Gotta Shoe* (cast recording). Available on CD
December 1975, *Elisabeth Welch*
June 1976, *Soft Lights and Sweet Music*
January 1980, *Aladdin* (cast recording)
July 1985, *Jerome Kern Goes to Hollywood* (cast recording)
May 1986, *Where Have You Been?* (New York). Available on CD
August 1986, *Elisabeth Welch in Concert.* Available on CD
September 1986, *In with the Old* (cast recording)
April 1987, *Elisabeth Welch Sings Irving Berlin Songbook.* Available on CD
January 1989, *This Thing Called Love.* Available on CD
May 1989, *Cole Porter's Nymph Errant* (recorded live at the Theatre Royal, Drury Lane)
July 1989, *Elisabeth Welch Sings Jerome Kern Songbook.* Available on CD
October 1989, *Elisabeth Welch Live in New York.* Available on CD
March 1990, *A Little Night Music* (cast recording). Available on CD
June 1991, *Cole Porter Centennial Gala* (recorded live at the Prince Edward Theatre)

Compilations
1979   *Miss Elisabeth Welch 1933–1940*
1993   *Paul Robeson & Elisabeth Welch: Songs from Their Films.* Available on CD
1995   *Elisabeth Welch "Soft Lights and Sweet Music."* Available on CD
2001   *Elisabeth Welch "Harlem in My Heart."* Available on CD

Salute to Malta

In 1942 Elisabeth contributed to a specially recorded disc called *Salute to Malta*, described in the introduction as "an informal programme of entertainment recorded by friends in London as a small expression of the gratitude and admiration which we at home in Britain feel towards the gallant garrison and people of the island of Malta." Following Laurence Olivier's reading of "a poem for Malta," Elisabeth performed Harold Arlen and Johnny Mercer's "Blues in the Night." Others who took part included Stanley Holloway, Carroll Gibbons, Leslie Henson, Jack Hulbert, Cicely Courtneidge, Diana Wynyard, Tommy Trinder, and Evelyn Laye.

Awards and Tributes

Incredible as it may seem, Elisabeth was over eighty before she was nominated for an award and eighty-two when she finally received one.

1985 This Is Your Life
On November 6, 1985, on British television, Elisabeth was the subject of *This Is Your Life*.

1985 Laurence Olivier Awards
Elisabeth was nominated for Britain's most prestigious theatre award in the category of Outstanding Performance by an Actress in a Musical for *Kern Goes to Hollywood*. The award went to Patti Lupone *(The Cradle Will Rock* and *Les Miserables)*; the other nominees were Betsy Brantley *(Guys and Dolls)* and Carol Sloman *(Lennon)*. Elisabeth attended the ceremony, which took place on December 8, 1985, at the Dominion Theatre in London's West End.

1986 Obie
On May 19, 1986, for *Time to Start Living*, Elisabeth received an Obie award for "Outstanding achievement in Off-Broadway theatre." The *Village Voice* Obie awards were created soon after the inception of the publication in 1955 to acknowledge publicly and encourage the growing Off-Broadway theatre movement.

1986 Outer Critics Circle
On May 22, 1986, for *Time to Start Living*, Elisabeth was presented with a special award by members of the Outer Critics Circle "for making old song favorites young, fresh, and vital." The presentation took place at Sardi's Eugenia Room in New York.

1985–1986 Drama Desk
For *Time to Start Living*, Elisabeth was nominated for a Drama Desk award for "Outstanding One Person Show." These cover *all* New York theatre productions, not just Broadway. The presentation took place on May 29, 1986.

1985–1986 Tony Awards

Elisabeth was nominated for America's most prestigious theatre honour, the Antoinette Perry "Tony" award, in the category of Featured Actress in a Musical for *Jerome Kern Goes to Hollywood*. The award went to Bebe Neuwirth (*Sweet Charity*); the other nominees were Patti Cohenour (*The Mystery of Edwin Drood*) and Jana Schneider (*The Mystery of Edwin Drood*). Elisabeth's friend Cleo Laine was also nominated that year in the category of Actress in a Musical for *The Mystery of Edwin Drood*, but she lost to Bernadette Peters (*Song and Dance*). Elisabeth attended the ceremony, which took place on June 1, 1986, at the Minskoff Theatre in New York. The Tony Awards were telecast live in the United States on CBS-TV.

1988 Variety Club of Great Britain

On February 7, 1989, Elisabeth received a special award for "Services to Entertainment" from the Variety Club of Great Britain at the presentation of their 1988 honours. The ceremony took place at the London Hilton Hotel and was televised later that day on BBC1.

1989 Black Filmmakers Hall of Fame

On February 26, 1989, Elisabeth was presented with the Black Filmmakers Hall of Fame award by Danny Glover and Beverly Todd at the Sixteenth Annual Oscar Micheaux Awards Ceremony at the Oakland Paramount Theatre of the Arts in Oakland, California. Elisabeth was absent, but an acceptance speech taped in London was broadcast (with extracts from *Song of Freedom* and *Keeping Love Alive*) during the ceremony. This was televised in the United States on May 28, 1989. The award was sent to England and presented to Elisabeth by Stephen Bourne and David Robinson on June 22, 1990, at the British Film Institute in London.

From 1974 to 1989 the Black Filmmakers Hall of Fame honoured over one hundred film personnel, including actors, producers, writers, and directors, but Elisabeth was the only recipient to be given an award for appearances in British films. Past recipients had included several who had been associated with Elisabeth and are mentioned in this book: Paul Robeson (1974), Lena Horne (1975), Fredi Washington (1975), Josephine Baker (1976), Eubie Blake (1976), Ethel Waters (1976), Benny Carter (1978), Nina Mae McKinney (1978), Bill "Bojangles" Robinson (1978), and Cab Calloway (1982).

1989 Cabaret Classics

On October 19, 1989, Elisabeth received, along with Bobby Short, Sylvia Syms, Margaret Whiting, Julie Wilson, and Hildegarde, a Cabaret Classic award at the first Cabaret Convention, sponsored by The Mabel Mercer Foundation. The ceremony took place at New York's Town Hall, and Elisabeth received a crystal G-sharp note engraved with her name.

1991 **BASCA**
On October 10, 1991, Elisabeth was presented with the BASCA (British Academy of Songwriters, Composers, and Authors) Gold Badge of Merit Award at the London Hilton Hotel. Other recipients that year included Shirley Bassey, Gerry Marsden (of Gerry and the Pacemakers), Richard O'Brien (of *Rocky Horror Show* fame), Helen Shapiro, Dorothy Squires, and Marty Wilde.

1992 **The Gallery First-Nighters**
On April 26, 1992, The Gallery First Nighters' Club gave a special dinner in honour of Elisabeth at the London Marriott Hotel. Cleo Laine and Evelyn Laye were among the guests.

1992 **A Time to Start Living**
On December 6, 1992, Elisabeth took part in *A Time to Start Living: A Celebration of the Great Elisabeth Welch*, a World AIDS Day all-star tribute in her honour, at The Lyric Theatre, Shaftesbury Avenue. The following description of the tribute was written by Ken Sephton, who first saw Elisabeth in *Happy and Glorious* in 1945:

> This tribute to the legendary Elisabeth Welch was an evening of highlights and one of the best star concerts I have attended. Directed and devised by David Kernan it was hosted by the urbane and witty Ned Sherrin introducing each item with a link to Elisabeth's life and long career. She entered the stage box to a rousing welcome and watched from there.
>
> The show began with a lively version of "The Song Is You" by Claire Moore, Michael Howe and Liz Robertson, followed by "Follow Me," a gospel song from members of the cast of *Carmen Jones*. Maria Friedman sang a haunting version of "Little Girl Blue" and was joined by Claire Moore and Louise Gold for a rousing "The Lady is a Tramp." Marion Montgomery did a leisurely "It Never Entered My Mind" and Angela Richards started "Ten Cents a Dance" by sitting down wearily, throwing off a shoe and massaging her foot! This was on the same stage where she made her name twenty-eight years ago in *Robert and Elizabeth*.
>
> The Irving Davies dancers awash with Folies Bergère plumage sang and danced "Bonjour Paris" before being joined by Josephine Blake sleek and slinkily working her way through "I Love Paris" and "Milord." Then *les girls* ended this sequence with "Can Can." Joanne Campbell recreated Josephine Baker's famous song *"J'ai Deux Amours"* and Petula Clark, after a song in French, said "I'm still known there as Petu La Clark!" then introduced a ballet for three dancers to "Love for Sale."

Louise Gold found a new interpretation of "The Physician" from *Nymph Errant* while Martin Smith played and sang "I Gaze in Your Eyes" from *A Swell Party*. Sam Harris, a young man unknown to me, brought the house down with a rip-roaring "Blow Gabriel, Blow."

Fenella Fielding performed the hilarious "Damsel in Distress" which Lis had introduced in revue, and then Peter Greenwell played and sang "A Nightingale Sang in Berkeley Square." From Peter's musical *The Crooked Mile*, Millicent Martin and Julia McKenzie gave a novel twist to "Meet the Family" aided by two Chippendale-style dancers, one black, one white, who proceeded to striptease, which greatly teased the audience.

Paul Jones, accompanying himself on the harmonica, gave us "Magic to Do" followed by Brent Barrett with "Corner of the Sky." These two songs came from *Pippin*. Robin Cousins abandoned his skates for the occasion to sing and dance a lively "I Won't Dance" with Bonnie Langford, and then the enchanting Sally Ann Howes held the audience spellbound with tender versions of "Yesterdays" and "Smoke Gets in Your Eyes." Elaine Delmar and Liz Robertson combined "Can't Help Lovin' That Man" and "Bill" from *Show Boat* in a clever and pleasing arrangement. The first half ended with Simon Green, David Kernan and Mark Wynter delighting us with "Song of the Sand" from *La Cage aux Folles*.

In the interval I eavesdropped on Chita Rivera, Sheridan Morley, Faith Brook, Derek Jacobi and Margaret Courtenay raving about the show.

The second-half had a night-club setting with members of the cast seated at tables providing an enthusiastic support for the cabaret which began with John Dankworth and Cleo Laine performing "My Cousin from Milwaukee," "Why Was I Born?" and "Stormy Weather" plus some unrehearsed banter! Bobby Short flew over from New York to make his West End debut giving us "I've Got My Eyes on You," "Drop Me Off in Harlem," "Body and Soul" and "Just One of Those Things" as only he can. Despite a husky throat, he showed us why he is known as The King of Piano Entertainers.

Then to round off a marvellous party the lady herself showed us what style is with her perfect renditions of "The Nearness of You," "*La Vie en Rose,*" "Solomon," "As Time Goes By" (which she was singing for a decade before the film *Casablanca* came out!), "No Time at All" and "It Had to Be You," interrupted by amusing chat with the host, the artists on stage and the adoring audience. The show over-ran nearly forty-five minutes but nobody minded because we had savoured one of those rare evenings when all was perfect, the music, the performances in a packed house, paying tribute to a great lady.

1994 **National Film Theatre**

From December 7 to 28, 1994, *Soft Lights and Sweet Music*, a retrospective of Elisabeth's film and television career, was compiled by Stephen Bourne for London's National Film Theatre. Screenings included *Song of Freedom* (1936),

Big Fella (1937), Over the Moon (1937), Alibi (1942), Mrs Patterson (TV 1956), The Rise and Fall of Nellie Brown (TV 1964), The Long Cocktail Party (TV 1966), and Paul Robeson (TV 1978), with extracts from Death at Broadcasting House (1934), Soft Lights and Sweet Music (1936), Calling All Stars (1937), Television Is Here Again (1946), Music for You (TV 1956), Not So Much a Programme, More a Way of Life (TV 1965 with Cleo Laine), The Tempest (1979), and Wogan (TV 1985 and 1990 with Terry Wogan). On December 11, following a screening of Keeping Love Alive (1987), Elisabeth was interviewed on stage by the film's co-director, David Robinson. It was one of her last public appearances.

~

Cast List

Adrian, Max, 1903–1973. Irish-born actor, partner of the actor and director, Laurier Lister; with EW in three Lister revues, *Tuppence Coloured* (1947), *Oranges and Lemons* (1948) and *Penny Plain* (1951).

Arlen, Harold, 1905–1986. American composer of "Stormy Weather" which EW introduced to Britain in 1933 and performed in Derek Jarman's *The Tempest* (1979).

Ashcroft, Peggy, 1907–1991. British actress; with EW in the Paul Robeson Memorial Concert and A Tribute to Michael Redgrave (both 1985).

Baddeley, Hermione, 1906–1986. British actress; with EW in *Sky High* (1942). Made guest appearance in EW's *This Is Your Life* (1985).

Baker, Josephine, 1906–1975. African American entertainer; with EW in *The Chocolate Dandies* (1924).

Beaumont, Hugh "Binkie," 1908–1973. Welsh producer and managing director of H. M. Tennent Ltd. EW was a member of the troupe he sent to Gibraltar to entertain the troops (1942–1943).

Bricktop (Ada Beatrice Queen Victoria Louise Virginia Smith du Conge), 1894–1984. African American entertainer who employed EW at Bricktop's, her famous Paris nightclub, in the early 1930s.

Bruce, Esther, 1912–1994. Black British seamstress who made dresses for EW from 1935 to 1941.

Calloway, Cab, 1907–1994. African American bandleader and entertainer; with EW at the London Palladium (1934).

Carter, Benny, 1907–2003. African American jazz musician; he recorded with EW in London in 1936 and composed the music for "Nightfall," performed by EW in *Calling All Stars* (1937).

Cavalcanti, Alberto, 1897–1982. Brazilian director; directed EW in *Dead of Night* (1945).

Cochran, Charles B., 1872–1951. British impresario; EW made her first major London appearance in Cochran's *Nymph Errant* (1933).

Coward, Noël, 1899–1973. British actor, playwright, composer and director; in 1969 EW took part in his seventieth-birthday tribute and performed his "Twentieth Century Blues."

Dolin, Anton, 1904–1983. British-Irish dancer and choreographer; with EW in *All the Best* (1938).

Ellis, Mary, 1897–2003. American actress and singer; with EW in two Ivor Novello musicals: *Glamorous Night* (1935) and *Arc de Triomphe* (1943). Made guest appearance in EW's *This Is Your Life* (1985).

Evans, Edith, 1888–1976. British actress; with EW as a member of John Gielgud's troupe sent to Gibraltar to entertain the troops (1942–1943). Also with EW in a BBC radio adaptation of Ronald Firbank's *The Princess Zoubaroff* (1962).

Foresythe, Reginald, 1907–1958. British jazz composer of West African descent; EW's accompanist in 1930s and 1940s.

Fosse, Bob, 1927–1987. Oscar-winning American director and choreographer. Directed EW in London version of *Pippin* (1973).

Gielgud, John, 1904–2000. British actor; EW was a member of his troupe sent to Gibraltar to entertain the troops (1942–1943). Reunited with EW for *A Tribute to Michael Redgrave* at the Old Vic (1985).

Gingold, Hermione, 1897–1987. British actress; with EW in *Sky High* (1942).

Greenwell, Peter, b. (?). British composer; wrote the music for *The Crooked Mile* (1959) and accompanied EW at her first "audition" for *Pippin* (1973).

Grenfell, Joyce, 1910–1979. British actress and singer; with EW in *Tuppence Coloured* (1947) and *Penny Plain* (1951). Also with EW on BBC television in *Joyce Grenfell Requests the Pleasure* (1956).

Hall, Adelaide, 1901–1993. African American singer; with EW on Broadway in *Runnin' Wild* (1923) and *Blackbirds of 1928*. Also with EW in Paris at the Moulin Rouge in *Blackbirds* (1929), in New York in *Black Broadway* (1980), and in London in the *Cole Porter Centennial Gala* (1991). Made guest appearance in EW's *This Is Your Life* (1985).

Harrison, Rex, 1908–1990.   British actor; with EW in *No Time for Comedy* (1941).

Horne, Lena, b. 1917.   African American singer; sang "Stormy Weather" in film of the same name in 1943. Made guest appearance in EW's *This Is Your Life* (1985).

Hunter, Alberta, 1895–1984.   African American blues singer and songwriter; friend of EW.

Hurst, Brian Desmond, 1895–1986.   British director; friend and neighbour of EW who directed her in *Alibi* (1942).

Jarman, Derek, 1942–1994.   British filmmaker, artist, writer; directed EW in *The Tempest* (1979).

Kitt, Eartha, b. 1927.   African American actress and singer; with EW in BBC television's *Mrs. Patterson* (1956).

Laine, Cleo, b. 1927.   British singer; with EW on stage (1962) and television (1966) in *Cindy-Ella*. Made guest appearance in EW's *This Is Your Life* (1985) and took part in all-star tribute to EW (1992).

Lawrence, Gertrude, 1898–1952.   British actress and singer; with EW in *Nymph Errant* (1933).

Laye, Evelyn, 1900–1996.   British actress and musical comedy star; made guest appearance in EW's *This Is Your Life* (1985).

Lillie, Beatrice (Lady Peel), 1894–1989.   Canadian-born revue artist; with EW as a member of John Gielgud's troupe sent to Gibraltar to entertain the troops (1942–1943).

Lister, Laurier, 1907–1986.   Actor, author, manager, and director; devised and directed three EW revues: *Tuppence Coloured* (1947), *Oranges and Lemons* (1948), and *Penny Plain* (1951).

Mack, Cecil (Richard C. McPherson), 1883–1944.   African American lyricist and choirmaster. Wrote the lyrics to "Charleston," which EW launched in *Runnin' Wild* (1923). EW joined his choir, which then made its debut in *Blackbirds of 1928*.

Martin, Millicent, b. 1934.   British actress and singer; with EW in *The Crooked Mile* (1959) and on BBC television in *The Long Cocktail Party* (1966). Took part in all-star tribute to EW (1992).

Mercer, Mabel, 1900–1984.   British singer. Friend of EW.

Novello, Ivor, 1893–1951.   Welsh actor-manager and composer; EW appeared in Novello's *Glamorous Night* (1935) and *Arc de Triomphe* (1943).

Piaf, Edith, 1915–1963.   French cabaret singer and songwriter; EW introduced Piaf's *"La Vie en Rose"* to Britain in 1947 and for BBC Radio 2 narrated the series *Portrait of Piaf* (1976).

Porter, Cole, 1891–1964.   American composer and lyricist; EW appeared in Porter's *The New Yorkers* (1931) and *Nymph Errant* (1933).

Redgrave, Michael, 1908–1985.   British actor; with EW in *Dead of Night* (1945).

Robeson, Paul, 1898–1976.   African American actor and singer; with EW in two films: *Song of Freedom* (1936) and *Big Fella* (1937).

Robinson, Bill, 1878–1949.   African American dancer; with EW on Broadway in *Blackbirds of 1928*.

Robinson, David, b. 1930.   British film critic and historian; directed EW in the documentary *Keeping Love Alive* (1987) and interviewed her on-stage at the Riverside Studios (1989) and National Film Theatre (1994).

Sherrin, Ned, b. 1931.   British producer; associated with EW from the 1950s. Hosted an all-star tribute to EW (1992).

Short, Bobby, b. 1926–2005.   African American cabaret entertainer; appeared with EW in *Black Broadway* (New York, 1980) and *A Time to Start Living* (London, 1992).

Smith, Luke, 1890s–1936.   African American musician. Brother of Joe Smith, Bessie Smith's favourite accompanist. Married to EW from 1928 to 1936.

Trinder, Tommy, 1909–1989.   British comedian; with EW in the film *Fiddlers Three* (1944) and revue *Happy and Glorious* (1944–1946). Made a guest appearance in EW's *This Is Your Life* (1985).

Waters, Ethel, 1896–1977.   African American actress and singer; introduced "Stormy Weather" at the Cotton Club in 1933. Met EW in Paris, 1929.

Wildeblood, Peter, 1923–1999.   British-Canadian journalist, novelist, playwright, and gay rights campaigner; wrote the book and lyrics for *The Crooked Mile* (1959).

Wills, James Elder, 1900–1970.   British director; directed EW in *Song of Freedom* (1936) and *Big Fella* (1937).

Bibliography

Bourne, Stephen. *Black in the British Frame: The Black Experience in British Film and Television.* London: Continuum, 2001.

———. "Elisabeth Welch: A Touch of Class." *Classic Images*, January 2000.

———. "Pauline Henriques" (obituary). *Independent*, November 21, 1998.

———. *Sophisticated Lady: A Celebration of Adelaide Hall.* London: ECOHP (Ethnic Communities Oral History Project), 2001.

Bourne, Stephen, and Esther Bruce. *Aunt Esther's Story.* London: ECOHP (Ethnic Communities Oral History Project), 1996.

Brahms, Caryl, and Ned Sherrin. *Cindy-Ella or I Gotta Shoe.* London: W. H. Allen, 1962.

Cameron, Kenneth M. *Africa on Film: Beyond Black and White.* New York: Continuum, 1994.

Cameron Williams, Iain. *Underneath a Harlem Moon: The Harlem to Paris Years of Adelaide Hall.* London: Continuum, 2002.

Cripps, Thomas. *Slow Fade to Black: The Negro in American Film, 1900–1942.* Oxford: Oxford University Press, 1977.

Egan, Bill. *Florence Mills: Harlem Jazz Queen.* Lanham, Md.: Scarecrow, 2004.

Ellis, Mary. *Those Dancing Years: The Autobiography of Mary Ellis.* London: John Murray, 1982.

Fawkes, Richard. *Fighting for a Laugh: Entertaining the British and American Armed Forces 1939–1946.* London: Macdonald and Jane's, 1978.

Feingold, Michael. "Born to Float." *Village Voice*, April 1, 1986.

Gielgud, John. "Christmas Party in Gibraltar." *Theatre Arts*, May 1943.

Gould, Robert. *A Touch of Practical Magic.* London: Longman Young Books, 1973.

Green, Jeffrey. "High Society and Black Entertainers in the 1920s and 1930s." *New Community*, Spring 1987.

———. "The Negro Renaissance in England." In *Black Music in the Harlem Renaissance*, edited by Samuel A. Floyd, Jr. New York: Greenwood, 1990.

Green, Stanley. *Encyclopaedia of the Musical*. London: Cassell, 1976.

Grenfell, Joyce. *Joyce Grenfell Requests the Pleasure*. London: Hodder and Stoughton, 1976.

Hammond, Bryan, and Patrick O'Connor. *Josephine Baker*. London: Jonathan Cape, 1988.

Hughes, Langston. *The Big Sea*. New York: Knopf, 1940.

Hughes, Langston, and Milton Meltzer. *Black Magic: A Pictorial History of the African-American in the Performing Arts*. New York: Da Capo, 1967.

Hurst, Brian Desmond. Travelling the Road. Unpublished autobiography, 1986.

Jablonski, Edward. *Harold Arlen: Happy with the Blues*. New York: Da Capo, 1961.

Jarman, Derek. *Dancing Ledge*. London: Quartet Books, 1984.

Johnson, James Weldon. *Black Manhattan*. New York: Knopf, 1930.

Kimball, Robert, and William Bolcom. *Reminiscing with Sissle and Blake*. New York: Viking, 1973.

Laine, Cleo. *Cleo*. London: Simon and Schuster, 1994.

Lida, David. "The Return of an American Diva." *Women's Wear Daily*, January 28, 1986.

Lumet Buckley, Gail. *The Hornes: An American Family*. London: Weidenfeld and Nicholson, 1987.

Mangan, Richard, ed. *Gielgud's Letters*. London: Weidenfeld and Nicholson, 2004.

Mapp, Edward. *Directory of Blacks in the Performing Arts*. 2d ed. Metuchen, N.J.: Scarecrow, 1990.

McBrien, William. *Cole Porter: The Definitive Biography*. London: HarperCollins, 1998.

McFarlane, Brian. *The Encyclopedia of British Film*. London: Methuen/British Film Institute, 2003.

McHugh, Fionnuala. "Sixty years and Still in Good Voice." *Times* (London), December 17, 1987.

McVay, Douglas. *The Musical Film*. London: A. Zwemmer, 1967.

Melly, George. "Cole's Nymph Errant." *Independent Magazine*, May 13, 1989.

Morgan, Thomas L., and William Barlow. *From Cakewalks to Concert Halls: An Illustrated History of African American Popular Music from 1895 to 1930*. Washington D.C.: Elliott and Clark, 1992.

Noble, Peter. *The Negro in Films*. London: Skelton Robinson, 1948.

O'Brien, Geraldine. "Lost Girlie Survives with Grace." *Sydney Morning Herald*, January 30, 1988.

O'Connor, Patrick. "Conversation Piece." *Connoisseur*, July 1987.

Parker, Derek, and Julia Parker. *The Story and the Song: A Survey of English Musical Plays 1916–78*. London: Chappel/Elm Tree Books, 1979.

Peake, Tony. *Derek Jarman*. London: Little, Brown, 1999.

Pick, Michael. "Solomon's Mines." *Antiques International*, Summer 1996.

Pines, Jim, ed. *Black and White in Colour: Black People in British Television since 1936*. London: British Film Institute, 1992. (Includes Stephen Bourne's interview with Elisabeth Welch.)

Robbins, Christopher. *The Empress of Ireland: Chronicle of an Unusual Friendship*. London: Scribner/Simon and Schuster, 2004.

Robinson, David. "A Woman with Something to Sing About." *Times* (London), June 18, 1983.

Sampson, Henry T. *Blacks in Blackface: A Source Book on Early Black Musical Shows*. Metuchen, N.J.: Scarecrow, 1980.

Short, Bobby. *Bobby Short: The Life and Times of a Saloon Singer*. With Robert Mac-Kintosh. New York: Clarkson Potter, 1995.

Simpson, Jim. "Elisabeth Welch in Conversation." *Overtures*, March 1981.

Slide, Anthony. "Elisabeth Welch." *Films in Review*, October 1987.

Thompson, Leslie. *Leslie Thompson: An Autobiography*. As told to Jeffrey Green. Crawley, England: Rabbit, 1985.

Waters, Ethel, with Charles Samuels. *His Eye Is on the Sparrow*. London: W. H. Allen, 1951.

Webb, Paul. *Ivor Novello: Portrait of a Star*. London: Stage Directions, 1999.

Welch, Elisabeth. "Memories of Cole." *Sunday Telegraph*, June 2, 1991.

———. "A Night to Remember." *Sunday Telegraph*, November 29, 1992.

Woll, Allen. *Black Musical Theatre: From Coontown to Dreamgirls*. Baton Rouge: Louisiana State University Press, 1989.

Index

Names

Addinsell, Richard, 65
Adrian, Max, 63, 65–66, 68, 76, 96
Agate, James, xii, 41
Alexander, Michael, 1–2, 64, 68, 70, 78, 88
Anderson, Ivie, 32
Anderson, Lindsay, 94–95
Andrews, Eamon, 91
Arlen, Harold, 31
Armstrong, Louis, 35, 87
Ashcroft, Peggy, 50, 67, 84
Ashton, Frederick, 81
Astor, David, xxv
Astor, Nancy, xxv
Attenborough, Richard, 67
Attille, Martina, 110
Attles, Joe, 98

Baddeley, Hermione, 54, 91
Bailey, Pearl, 73
Baker, Josephine, xii, xvii, 10–12, 17, 19, 37, 49, 54, 73, 103
Baptiste, Thomas, 74

Basie, Count, 73
Bassey, Shirley, 75, 105–8
Bates, Alan, 110
Beaumont, Hugh (Binkie), 56
Belafonte, Harry, 61
Bennett, Joan, 72
Bennett, Tony, 73
Berlin, Irving, xii, 24, 27, 64, 93–94, 97, 99
Bethune, Dr. Mary McLeod, 103
Bevan, Tim, xxiii
Black, George, 41
Blackwood, Maureen, 110
Blake, Eubie, 7, 10–11
Boulaye, Patti, 108
Boyd, Stephen, 72
Bradley, Buddy, 33
Brahms, Caryl, 74, 76
Braun, Eric, 80
Bricktop, xii, 20, 73
Brockhurst, Gerald, xx
Brown, Lawrence, 48
Browne, George, 74–77
Bruce, Esther, xviii–xix, xxi
Bubbles, John W., 87

143

Gilbert, W. Stephen, 95
Gingold, Hermione, xx, 54, 59–60, 94
Goetz, E. Ray, 24, 99
Gould, Robert, 75
Granger, Derek, xxv, 103
Grant, Cy, 74–76
Graves, Peter, 54, 91
Gray, Dolores, 67, 94
Green, Adolph, 97
Green, Jeffrey, 32–33
Greenaway, Peter, 84
Greene, Graham, 46
Greenwell, Peter, xii, 70–71, 76, 78
Grenfell, Joyce, 63, 65–68, 96

Hall, Adelaide, 10, 12–14, 17, 21, 38,
    51, 55, 87, 91
Hall, Henry, 36–37, 41
Hamilton, Ord, 39
Hammerstein, Oscar, II, 43
Hammond, Bryan, 11, 96
Hammond, Kay, 52, 67
Hare, Doris, 53
Harrison, Rex, 53, 72
Hart, Lorenz, xix, 68, 92–93, 97
Hassall, Christopher, 27–28
Hayter, James, 48
Hemingway, Ernest, 20
Henriques, Pauline, xviii
Hepburn, Katharine, 110
Heyward, Du Bose, 12
Hill, Rose, 66
Hines, Gregory, 88
Holiday, Billie, 15, 20
Holloway, Stanley, 41, 67
Hope, Bob, 110
Horne, Lena, xvii, 13, 15, 31, 61, 73,
    91–92
Howes, Sally Ann, xvii
Hughes, Langston, 10, 20
Hughes, Revella, 98
Hunter, Alberta, 32, 38, 69, 77, 106
Hurst, Brian Desmond, xx, 30, 59, 60

Hurston, Zora Neale, 103
Hutchinson, Leslie (Hutch), 33–34

Ivaldi, Alfredo, xxi

Jackson, Delilah, 98–99
Jacobs, John, 75
Jarman, Derek, xiii, xix, xxii–xxiii, 30,
    61–62, 79, 81–87, 89–90
Jean-Baptiste, Marianne, 105
John, Errol, 75
Johnson, James P., 7
Johnson, James Weldon, 7
Johnson, Ken (Snakehips), 38
Jolson, Al, 44, 73
Jones, Griffith, 58
Jones, Paul, 78, 91
Joyce, Peggy Hopkins, 23
Julien, Isaac, xxiv

Kay, Elisabeth. See Welsh, Elisabeth
Kempson, Rachel, 84
Kendall, Kay, 54
Kern, Jerome, xxiv, 28, 43, 88–91, 93,
    97
Kernan, David, xiii, xvii, 76, 79, 88–89
Kitt, Eartha, 39, 68–69, 73, 109
Knight, Gladys, 108
Koehler, Ted, 31
Korda, Alexander, 40, 44
Kreuger, Miles, 102

Laine, Cleo, xii, xvii, 49, 68, 70, 74–76,
    91, 93, 105–7
Lawley, Sue, 99
Lawrence, Gertrude, xvii–xviii, 25–27,
    29, 89, 96
Laye, Evelyn, xix, 52, 67, 91
Layton and Johnstone, 33
Layton, Turner, 39, 55
Le Gon, Jeni, 106
Leigh, Vivien, 52
Lennon, John, 97

Theatre

Concerts

Songs

About the Author

Stephen Bourne is one of Britain's leading authorities on black history. He is a regular contributor to *Black Filmmaker* magazine and the author of *Aunt Esther's Story* (1996, a biography of his aunt, a black seamstress born in London before the First World War), *A Ship and a Prayer* (1999), *Black in the British Frame: The Black Experience in British Film and Television* (second edition, Continuum, 2001), and *Sophisticated Lady: A Celebration of Adelaide Hall* (2001). He has organised many film and television events for the National Film Theatre in London, including retrospectives dedicated to the careers of Ethel Waters (1993), Elisabeth Welch (1994), Anna May Wong (1995), and Paul Robeson (1998). For British television he was a researcher on Channel 4's *Sophisticated Lady* (1989, a profile of Adelaide Hall), Channel 4's *We Sing and We Dance* (1992, a profile of the Nicholas Brothers), and BBC-2's *Black and White in Colour* (1992, a two-part history of black people in British television). For the BBC's Windrush season in 1998, he researched and scripted Radio 2's *Their Long Voyage Home*. Stephen has been interviewed in several documentaries, including Channel 4's *Black Divas* (1996) and *Paul Robeson: Here I Stand* (1999, an *American Masters* presentation directed by St Clair Bourne). Stephen has received two Race in the Media awards from the Commission for Racial Equality, and for *Black in the British Frame* he was short-listed for *The Voice* newspaper's Black Community Award for Literature.